Undressing the N-word: Revealing the Naked Truth about Lies, Deceit and Mind Games, Copyright © 2014 by H. Lewis Smith

Cover & Interior Design, George Michael Rodrigues
Cover Concept, H. Lewis Smith

ISBN 978-0-615-96242-9

This book was printed in the United States of America.
To order additional copies of this book, visit: www.theunitedvoices.com
Email: admin@theunitedvoices.com

Undressing the N-word:

Revealing the Naked Truth about Lies, Deceit and Mind Games

By

H. Lewis Smith

This Book is Dedicated to

my daughters Tobin R. Smith and T. Sherriel Weithers; my grandsons Patrick Weithers, Pierre Lewis; and great-grandson Kadyn Xavier-Wayne Lewis.

In Loving Memory of

Shirley Ann Smith, kindred spirit and sister

Acknowledgements

I would like to acknowledge and thank family and friends who probed, encouraged and supported me in the writing of this book. I also extend my gratitude to Ashley Phoenix Business Solutions who did such a fine job on collaborating with UVCC to edit the manuscript of this work.

Contents

Introduction

"The Eurocentric educational philosophy will not provide you with the tools to conquer a system that oppresses you."
~Dr. Asa Hilliard (1933 – 2007)

In these contemporary times, the n-word (or n**ger, n**ga, or n**gah) has become an enigma that seems to now possess a different meaning to different people. Some use the term as a form of endearment, saying that they have changed the meaning of the word; others somehow have come to surmise that it is simply an empty term that no longer carries any power. Few understand or blatantly ignore the full significance, purpose and intent of the word. They seem to forget, remain ignorant to, or foolishly cackle at the fact that the term *is* more than *just* a word; it is, indeed, a psychological weapon that continues to slaughter the psyche and stagnate the progression of generation upon generation of Black/African Americans, and, ultimately, society as a whole.

In the following passages of *Undressing the N-word*, the naked, unadulterated truth is revealed. All of the lies, deceit, subliminal and apparent mind games, as well as the true hidden agenda of maintaining mental enslavement of—or control over—a race of people, the Black race, are unveiled. As the reader ingests the text on the pages, the entire hope is that the reader will not turn a blind eye to the content but instead will become an enlightened student of the literature and even more awakened to the seriousness of the issue. The full hope is that the reader will fully digest and understand the actual message and education being conveyed to then gain the tools required to help self and others first re-claim self-dignity, which will then lead to restoring the dignity of the race.

Moreover, if the reader questions any line of script in this text, the expectation and urging is that the reader will begin a personal quest for greater or confirmed knowledge that will lead him/her to find the *real* truth. In doing so, the reader will begin his/her journey to living a truly unshackled life physically and, most importantly, mentally...

The n-word, its origins and the connection to the past that it represents, has had tremendous lasting effects on the Black African American. In fact, when Blacks were enslaved, they were forced to hate themselves and as a continual reminder of the disgust they were to have for themselves, they were referred to as a separate, sub-human class: a n**ger; and simultaneously forced to self-ingest the term.

To this very day, many Blacks suffer from this broken state of being and are convinced that their past is empty, backward, shameful or totally negative. Anyone with this type of perspective on life will surely resist any attempt to revisit or connect with that past in apparent fear of what they may or may not find. As a result, such a person will have no true identity or real awareness of his/her culture or heritage, and, subsequently, will likely, whether they realize it or not at the time, despise, loathe self, or feel disjointed from the collective society to some degree.

This same person will refuse to consciously take seriously or relate to any cultural customs, and will not make any effort at validating "facts" discovered. They remain in the darkness, helpless and dependent. This broken or confused line of thinking, perhaps, explains why so many Black African Americans become self-hating individuals, living contradictions of their former proud selves. Many are in denial about their ancestral linkage to their Motherland of Africa, defending their stance with some ready-made pseudo-intellectual reasoning in efforts to legitimize their disavowal of their Motherland.

To effectively address the issue and finally put to rest any linkages to the mentality of being a n**ga/n**ger, Black African Americans must consciously and sub-consciously realize that past teachings to ancestors and African-American forefathers were not for their liberation. Rather, their *mis-education* was administered in a way to *keep Blacks in their so-called place*, and was and still is only in the best interest of the ruling class. History translates into "his-story"—the manner in which one understands or interprets history from his or her own perspective to his or her own benefit. Contemporary Blacks, those who are paying attention, are living witnesses as to how Black history has been—by "his-story"—distorted, misleading, deceptive and mind controlling.

Evidence all around the world suggests that Black civilizations were far more advanced than the images portrayed to the Black community by the ruling class. The ruling class would have African Americans believe that the Black experience is limited to huts, spears and jungle life with no trace of civility, culture, organization, and self-sufficiency, ultimately painting the white man as their saving grace. Research exposes this chronicle as a gross fabrication.

The true essence of Africa is "The Cradle of Civilization", from the beginnings of humanity to the rise and fall of its great civilizations. In fact, origin of the oldest human species was discovered in East Africa, Ethiopia. Evidence also suggests that all human beings derive from one source. This, of course, begs the question of why do all people look so different. For an explanation visit: The Incredible Journey (August 2011), http://www.youtube.com/watch?v=vwa6o-s1Yvs.

With the exception of the black man's image as presented by academics, the average Black African American knows very little, if anything at all, about his/her African heritage; and of what the student has learned, more than likely, has been misinformation. The American-born black man and woman are completely brainwashed beings who only know, recognize and comprehend or experience what their oppressor has decided for them. It is incumbent upon Black America— as a group—to liberate their minds from Eurocentric ideologies and realize or discover the real truth and knowledge that has not been shared with them.

Humankind is asked to believe that white people gratuitously developed Egypt and as an afterthought decided to develop Europe thousands of years later; and, while supposedly developing Egypt, they benevolently built a Sphinx with Afroid features. The Sphinx symbolizes a very rich and rewarding history of the Black civilization. Because frontiersman like Napoleon Bonaparte refused to accept the fact that those they thought to be savage, uncivilized hooligans were actually a civilized, intelligent people with developments far advanced beyond Europe's own societies', after the Sphinx had stood perfect in its creator's eye for centuries, he ordered his soldiers to shoot off the Afroid nose. Like many others on down the line of history, Napoleon refused to accept all that the Sphinx truly represents—cultural pride, strength, dynamism, resourcefulness, and intellectual prowess of a once thriving Black civilization.

For some common reason, standard practice has been to deface the Afroid features of Egyptian artifacts and statuettes, then later deceivingly create drawings of these same artifacts with European facial features. The defaced artifacts and statuettes are on display in Egyptian museums today, further contributing to the fabricated lies conceived to smother the existence of a people all in the name of honoring stolen legacies.

The Sphinx after Napoleon's soldiers shot off its nose.

Western civilization (Greco-Roman culture) begins somewhere around the 8th century BC. Alexander the Great invaded Egypt 332 BC leading to the eventual fall of Egypt. However, centuries before that period, after being invaded by Asians, Egypt gradually transformed from being a Black civilization to its present day situation.

From 5th century AD (including the Dark Ages, Middle Ages, the Renaissance and well into the 16th century AD), Black civilizations were thriving in Spain and Africa while European culture was experiencing its developmental stages. The Europeans were liberated from the Dark Ages by the Moors and Arabs, and obtained their knowledge on how to function as a civilization from those who came before them; these knowledgeable predecessors were Black-ruled civilizations. Around this same time, Africa was already experiencing its third Golden Age through the civilizations of Mali, Ghana and Songhai. The Great Pyramid and Sphinx were thousands of years old by this point in time. So *what happened* to these extraordinary civilizations? Answers are forthcoming within the pursuing chapters of this book...

The point of the preceding paragraphs is that Black African Americans have a glorious history with which to identify and relate. The oppressors realized this factor and the innate greatness that lives within African Americans' blood long ago. Yet, due to their fear and artificial, indignantly-gained superior standing, the oppressor would rather for Blacks to believe that slavery and a wild, uncivilized jungle life is their *ONLY* history. However, that is an unmitigated fabrication.

Since the African Diasporas movement, Black African Americans have been drawing nearer to re-discovering the types of successes their race of people once accomplished. During the early 1920's, Blacks developed their own sovereign community independent of whites. This 35-block community in Tulsa, Oklahoma, was often referred to as "Little Africa" or "Black Wall Street". Black Wall Street was a thriving community with beautiful colonial housing, schools, a bank, hospital, and proved to be home to many black businessmen who were multimillionaires. In fact, Blacks were experiencing a higher quality of life than the surrounding communities that resided within that city.

Racist whites despised the African Americans' success because they were threatened by it. Blacks were too independent as far as whites were concerned. As such, the white community decided to take matters into their own hands. After years of growth, the thriving and flourishing city-within-a-city was set afire and burned down to the ground on June 1, 1921.

Clearly, Black African Americans have the aptitude and ability to succeed. Blacks, as a group, must think of themselves in a more *positive* and *capable* light to achieve all things good again such as a Black Wall

Street. The societal issues that exist in America today *cannot* be solved by the type of thinking that created them. Therefore, it is incumbent upon African Americans to *free* their *own* minds and see the world from a different, more upright perspective. In so doing, Black America will be able to resolve certain issues, which will then allow the Black community to again truly experience their greatest potential.

This can only be accomplished through economic independence, and the only way this level of economic independence and communal self-sufficiency can be attained is if Black America re-unites as ONE collective body to re-establish itself on a rock-solid foundation of cultural respect, awareness, dignity, class, and a highly-appraised collective self-worth. Within this book, the essential and fundamental necessity to eliminate use of the n-word from everyone's speech, heart, mind and soul in attaining this endeavor will be explained.

Secular and non-secular people who have spent centuries strategically and heinously orchestrating the Black community's physical, psychological, emotional and spiritual enslavement are not going to just turn around and set Blacks free. Blacks must remove the shackles of *mental enslavement* themselves; otherwise, *true* freedom is *never* going to happen.

The duty of restoring Blacks' prideful history as well as re-establishing a healthy self-image rests upon the shoulders of present day Black Americans. No one in the past can do it because they are long gone and the future generations have not yet arrived to handle this necessary call to action. As a strong believer in manifest destiny, this time in humanity's existence has been chosen or architected as *the* prime and crucial time for Black America to re-collect itself and progress for reasons that may not be wholly explainable right now.

Even still, it is clear that these duties must be carried out in the present. The requirement is incumbent upon the children of today; today's Black African Americans must take the reins and proclaim with conviction and honor as they ride out into this long but necessary journey: "It has begun with me!"

To be clear, the purpose of this book is not intended to be an indictment against white people in general; it is, instead, an indictment against an oppressing, biased system started by racist white people that has been in place for more than 400 years. The argument is against an institutionalized systemic that has become highly sophisticated; a racist systemic that many black and innocent white people alike are totally unaware of but exists nonetheless. This system is supported by the news media, academia, law enforcement, politicians, professional sports hierarchies, movie and music industries.

Furthermore, the intent of this book is to also not browbeat Black America or "air any dirty laundry." Truly, everything stated in the pages of this text is common knowledge. Black America is in a pivotal state at this point and it is up to each member of Black America, including myself, the writer of this book, to be accountable for and concerned about the outcome of Black America. Each African American must speak directly to the Black community about the existing issues to find resolve to these problems.

Any reader of this book must *not* use the contents to chastise the Black community or even think that ill is being spoken about the Black race. No! Rather, the reader—black or non-black, n-word supporter or anti-n-word advocate— must simply use this tool as an awakening mechanism and a foundation toward paving a tight-suited, balanced American society for the long-term. Martin Luther King once said, if one suffers, so all people suffer. Certainly, the ultimate objective is to end this suffering for all humanity, and this can be accomplished if Black African Americans hold one another accountable and responsible for each person's—black or non-black—own actions.

Back to it: the n-word is the epitome of negative energy. The objective is for African Americans to lead by example and *NOT* use the anathematized n-word themselves; after all, Black African Americans should be the last people on the face of this earth to be using the accursed term. To consider use of the term as cool, chic and/or a ridiculous so-called privilege extends beyond the scope of unimaginable, shameless stupidity.

The n-word serves as a link to the continual demise—or at least stagnant progression— and *mental enslavement* of the Black community. The contents of this book will clarify how the term continues to enslave the African American race to this very day. It will also disclose the real reasoning as to why black folks need to wake up and recognize that by continually breathing life into the term, they unknowingly are WILLING accomplices to their own demise. To drive home the importance and significance of this very important message, repetition and redundancy must and will prevail throughout this book.

PART I:

TO UNDERSTAND THE PRESENT,
BLACK AMERICA MUST NOT IGNORE THE PAST

Chapter 1

Massa's Creation of Slaves

"Capture their minds, and their hearts and souls will follow. For once their minds are reached, they're defeated without bullets."
~Anonymous

Visualize a circle roughly the size of a grapefruit. Imagine that the space inside this circle represents an individual's total, inclusive realm of knowledge. At the same time, this individual is also mindful that greater knowledge exists beyond their own particular circumference of awareness or current understanding. When a new piece of information—something outside this individual's existing circumference of awareness—is revealed to this person, it does not mean that the information is necessarily wrong, but it does mean that this is new information that the individual must somehow work to process. Whether the information is "good" or "bad," it will not be immediately accepted because it is *new* and must be assimilated to determine if it agrees or disagrees with one's current understanding.

It is a given and definitely a guarantee that the content of this book is going to be upsetting to some people as typically can be the truth for those who cannot handle it or stand to have their current knowledge base tested and expanded. Nonetheless, it is imperative to highlight how the African American community, on the whole— *from the most educated to the least educated*, have been programmed or conditioned to retaliate against and reject anything that sits outside their circle or circumference of awareness. They reject any new ideas without even hearing out or truly digesting the entire argument—particularly regarding the Black culture, the truth about the Black experience, and its effects upon the African American community's psyche.

The white man's account of the slave trade implies that blacks were selling blacks into slavery. An element of truth to this notion may very well exist, but it tells only half the story. The other half is that during that time period, slavery was not uncommon. Whites were enslaving whites and blacks were enslaving other blacks. Although all slavery was oppressive, slaves traded during periods prior to the American slave trade were treated far different from the slave experience America perpetuated upon the Africans. Not to their defense, but black slave sellers had no way of knowing that they were dealing with the most relentless enslavers. These black slave traders would unknowingly become willing participants in selling other blacks to an enslavement that subjected slaves to extremely harsh conditions and a dehumanization process beyond imagination. Such deplorable inhumane activities as chattel slavery were unheard of and unknown at the time.

American slavery, by law, classified slaves as "not to be ranked among sentient beings, but among things, as an article of property." This definition placed slaves at the level of brute animals.

Plantation owners, overseers, merchants, bankers—all of those who were benefactors of the American enslavement of African people—had a huge stake in eliminating the true identity of the newly-arrived Africans. These benefactors knew that in order for their scheme to be completely effective, they would have to maintain total control over the captives; the slaves would have to be resolutely obedient and loyal. They also realized that the slaves must be dependent on the slave masters for guidance, knowledge, and anything else that they needed so that slaves would never think

As a result of being tossed overboard, untold millions of enslaved Africans never survived the "Middle Passage" either due to deteriorating health or being too rebellious and defiant--unbreakable.

to rise up, revolt, and take back their God-given liberties. This objective could only be achieved if Africans were detached from their roots in every way and forced to live in an environment that would birth a warped mentality; thus, the required obedience, loyalty, and helplessness to create a good slave would be incubated and instilled from the start.

This newly-created image of a n**ga/n**ger was a childlike figure, often demonstrating infantile silliness and exaggeration no matter his age. Above all, though, the slave was to be and depicted as utterly dependent on and attached to his master. The master conveniently attributed the slave's submission to this state of being as inherent to the slave's race or his so-called primitive African culture. The slave master chose not to acknowledge that the mental abuse and physical torment the slave endured for decades was the driving factor that forced them into the embodiment of this ridiculed character.

Not only did White America become convinced of white superiority and black inferiority, but White America strove to impose these racial beliefs on the Africans themselves. Slave masters gave a great deal of attention to the *education* and *training* of the ideal slave and the creation of a n**ger/n**ga image. In general, five factors were the founding basis in molding the character and mind of such a slave. They were:

1. Exercising strict and harsh discipline against the slave.

2. Instilling a sense of self-worthlessness, hopelessness and inferiority in the enslaved so that they may NEVER, EVER FORGET their place as that of a n**ger/n**ga.

3. Believing in the master's so-called superior power.

4. Accepting and never questioning the master's standards and teachings.

5. Owning a deep sense of their (the slave's) own helplessness and dependence upon the master. Paternalism!

Once all of these factors were met with satisfaction, the indoctrination process of creating the *perfect slave,* physically and *mentally,* was now complete. As well, this particular process was not just a brief or current event for that moment in time. Rather, it planted seeds with deep roots that sadly ensured bountiful crops of mental enslavement for centuries to come. In this 21st century, many contemporary black users of the pejorative term serve as living proof to the success of this inculcation.

Subconsciously they have not been able to shake their prescribed so-called place as that of a n**ga/n**ger. They refuse to recognize the reality that they are carrying out a 400-year-old indoctrination process. It is a link in the chain of slavery from which many contemporary Blacks have been unable to free themselves. A weak, feeble mind is unable to rise above the orthodoxy; however, a stronger mind can. As such, the stronger, more stable-minded African Americans are going to have to help liberate the crippled minded ones from the anathematized 18th century slave mentality use of the n-word.

Enslaved Africans were stripped of their identities, given new names, and forced or coerced into believing that they and their African heritage was meaningless, inferior and barbaric. The enslaved were taught that all things good, significant, superior, and civil were of European descent. As a result, they eventually became completely dependent on and accepting of their masters' teachings as they had no other symbol or relation to self to which to cling. Slaves reluctantly began to voluntarily accept European values, traditions, and habits, unknowingly contributing to a total disintegration of the African culture.

Upon being stripped of his true identity and given a new name and image, the enslaved Black was taught to envision himself and his African heritage as inferior and barbaric. Paradoxically, the white man did not initially view the African as being inferior; the white man actually beheld and admired the achievements, progress, and civilization of the black man.

Nevertheless, because of his insecurities, the white power structure simply wished for Blacks to be inferior so that White America could maintain the myth of being the "superior" race. To maintain the "myth," they created the falsehood for all to believe, both Blacks and Whites alike, that the African was inherently inferior. This belief was imperative in order to justify the dehumanization, mental abuse, and enslavement process that was to ensue; and because they were able to carry out this enslavement and people bought into the dehumanization of Africans, their teachings were proven and taken as *the truth*.

The enslaved Black was stripped of his heritage so that no parts of his ingenious, dignified, self-reliant, culturally-aware and proud African background could influence his life in America. His personality, behavior, and self-image were re-shaped exclusively by the unique form of American slavery. This system of degradation birthed the exact opposite of what the enslaved Africans represented; the system birthed what was to be referred to as a n**ger/n**ga. The n**ger categorization was created to keep the enslaved African within a certain place of inferiority—mentally and socially; this inferior classification was established for consoling purposes relative to any and all misdeeds perpetrated upon the enslaved.

At the foundation of every teaching was the stressing and promoting of white superiority and black inferiority.

Besides teaching the slave to despise his own history and culture, the master strove to inculcate his own value system into the African's outlook. The white master insisted on total obedience and created a situation of utter dependence and *eternal paternalism*. He supplied food, clothing, shelter, discipline, and also granted himself the authority to determine who the slaves befriended and mated with as well.

The death rate among slaves was high. To replace their losses, plantation owners encouraged the slaves to have children. Indeed, slave farms existed in the South, primarily Virginia, where slave breeding was practiced. Slave breeding included coerced sexual relations between male and female slaves; promoted pregnancies of slaves, and sexual relations between master and slave with the aim of producing slave children. The rapist slave masters favored female slaves who produced a relatively large number of children, which culminated well into the tens of thousands. Child-bearing started around the age of thirteen, and by twenty the women slaves would be expected to birth four or five children. To encourage child-bearing, some plantation owners promised women slaves their freedom after they produced fifteen children. [1]

Suppose the pages of time were turned back. Consider the following question for a moment: if the enslaved Africans were as inferior as the slave masters insinuated, *why* did the need to indoctrinate, manipulate and browbeat the enslaved Africans into believing they were so inherently inferior exist? The only sensible explanation for White America's actions is that they were fearful of these remarkable people who had learned to survive and thrive through tilling the earth and using their own resources and intellect to develop a progressive society in their own right. White America was troubled and disturbed about those peculiar Africans who had developed an established society without Europeans.

Even more discerning to Europeans was the Africans' *initial* unwillingness to submit to servitude even after being beaten, mutilated, and humiliated. White slave traders and American slave owners knew that it would not be sufficient to only physically enslave the Africans; instead, they realized they had to also *defeat and control* them in *spirit* and in *mind*. Slave oppressors realized that if this plight was to work for the long-term, they had to urgently and effectively—through consistent practices— instill into the *hearts, minds and souls* of the enslaved Africans *fear* and an *inferiority complex.*

During chattel slavery, the slaves were first categorized before they were eventually humanized. Categorizing slaves as n**gers went far beyond the concept of a racial slur; it served as a psychological purpose to enslave their *minds*. To achieve this objective, some of the most brutal and inhumane methods were applied to dehumanize the enslaved, coercing them to accept a lower, valueless image of themselves. Through uncivilized and barbaric methods of abuse, the creation of the ideal slave was accomplished with resounding success.

The enslaved were conditioned to be intellectually childlike and paternalistic. They were programmed to think of and see themselves as being physically unattractive, lazy, stupid, dirty, worthless parasites who were ignorant and obsessively self-indulgent. They were told they were angry, physically strong, animalistic, and prone to wanton violence towards one another. During the course of a 400-year time frame, the enslaved and freed blacks were crudely browbeaten into assimilating this newly-created inferior status of themselves; this slave mentality is presently being passed down from generation to generation.

Through the physical and psychological trauma that was performed to actually create the ideal slave, two forms of enslavement prevailed: *physical* and *mental*. However, MENTAL enslavement is ultimately the worst, and to this very day, most Black African Americans have yet to be freed from its shackles and serves as a link to their present day social ills. This fact should *not* be taken lightly although attention is *never* drawn to it. The minds of the enslaved African Americans were *tinkered* and *toyed* with, *corrosively manipulated, abused* and *misused.*

One of the greatest powers in the world is the power to define reality and make others accept it, even when it's to their disadvantage. This manipulation occurred to the enslaved Africans and never arrested serves as a link to modern day African American's pathologies.

The Supreme Intelligence known to some as God created man. Though Blacks were re-programmed by a racist society to appraise themselves at lesser than their true worth, Blacks must, first, believe in their godliness to then accept and appreciate their god-like qualities— even including the most apparent features such as their eyes, lips, nose, skin-color, and so forth. Black people— just as all other races—are the children of the universe, no less than the stars and the trees. In so being, Blacks are no lesser than anyone else and no better; instead, all are equal. As such, Blacks were created by divine design, not by mistake. Black people have a right to be here and a reason for existing—which is not to serve as any other race's whipping post or laughing stalk. As individuals, black people must be grateful and learn to thank the Supreme Intelligence for making each person perfectly. In respecting and appreciating one's existence, Blacks must take back control of their *own* minds. This is an urgent imperative.

To understand present day issues that abound in the African American community requires one to retrieve the past so that the present may be better understood. By gaining this knowledge, the solutions to overcoming the prevailing issues will be made clear; then and only then will the community and society on a whole be able to proceed forward in a positive fashion. As the reader continues reading, he/she will find that the ensuing chapters present such an opportunity.

History has proven that even though African Americans did begin to adopt European values and ways of life for the most part, many Blacks continued to fight hard against the idea of being some insignificant sub-human unfit for descent living and entitlement to self-thought, self-fulfillment. For over three centuries, enslaved Africans were chastised, beaten, and tortured to accept a self-hating, self-destructing, self-abasing and self-abnegating image of self. Slaves' front teeth oftentimes were ripped out or broken off so that they could be easily detected if they ran away. They were frequently beaten severely and unmercifully, then red pepper would be rubbed into their lacerated flesh with hot salt water and spirits of turpentine poured over the gashes to increase the torture. They were often stripped naked to have their backs and limbs cut with knives, bruised and mangled by scores and hundreds of blows with a paddle and/or whip. Slaves were terribly torn by the claws of cats drawn over them by their tormentors, hunted with blood hounds and shot down like beasts, or torn to pieces by dogs. [2]

The slaves were often suspended in air by meat hooks, whipped and beaten until they fainted only to be revived to be beaten again until they fainted once again and sometimes died. Their ears were often cut off, eyes gouged out, bones broken, and flesh branded with red hot irons. They were maimed, mutilated and slowly burned to death over dawdling fires, serving as examples and a reminder to others to know and stay in their *appointed place* as that of a n**ger/n**ga.

This unfortunate victim was first castrated and then burnt alive.

All of the aforementioned cruel acts were often carried out with the ranting of "n**ger, n**ger, n**ger" ringing in the victim's ears. Tormentors believed their acts were justified. They had convinced themselves that in the eyesight of Jesus Christ and their Christian God, enslaved Africans were sub-humans (3/5 a person); that they were nothing more than valueless (animals) n**gers, and, therefore, any inhumane acts perpetrated upon them were acceptable.

Chapter 2

Undressing the N-word

If you can control a man's thinking you do not have to worry about his action. When you determine what a man shall think you do not have to concern yourself about what he will do. If you make a man feel that he is inferior, you do not have to compel him to accept an inferior status, for he will seek it himself. If you make a man think that he is justly an outcast, you do not have to order him to the back door. He will go without being told; and if there is no back door, his very nature will demand one.
~ Carter G. Woodson, "The Mis-Education of the Negro"

Forbiddingly, you learn today that your mother was brutally and unmercifully bludgeoned to death with a hammer. Now close your eyes and think about this for a moment: think about the heinousness in the act; see your mother screaming for her life and doing everything in her power to defend against and fight off her unrelenting attackers; think about all of the pain and anguish she endured as blow upon blow of the hammer welled down on her, before the final bit of life was unrightfully snatched with that last thud. Can you see it? Can you see the multiple plugs imprinted into whatever part of her body the hammer unforgivingly fell upon? Can you empathize with that dreadful moment in time?

Now ask yourself this: in order to memorialize your mother's life and honor her sacred and beautiful memory, would you start using a hammer as a symbol or in remembrance of your mother? Of course not! To the contrary, every time you saw a hammer, it would likely stir up strong feelings of sadness, disgust, and, perhaps, even hatred. The hammer would symbolize the bashing murder of your mom and, because of this association, you would elect to never disgrace her memory or embrace the cruel acts carried out against her by adopting the hammer as a symbol of the love and respect you possess for your mother. As a matter of fact, even if her murder occurred over 50 years ago, your feelings would not change and no one could convince you that a hammer is just a tool that carries no real power; rather, because of your experience, you would always view it as a weapon that unjustly ripped away a core part of who you are and someone that was most significant in your world.

In parallel to the previous analogy, replace the hammer with the term n**ger"; replace the mother figure with Black/African-American ancestors and present time Black America. The word n**ger (or n**ga or n**gah in ghetto vernacular) symbolizes death, terrorism and dehumanization in the lives of untold millions of Black people. Men, women, *and* children were butchered, slaughtered, severely beaten unmercifully, raped, disemboweled, and castrated all because they were considered valueless (animals) n**gers. They were murdered with the chant of "n**ger, n**ger, n**ger" ringing in their ears as they drew their last breaths.

Racial slurs such as *coon, jungle bunny, sambo, Uncle Tom, jigaboo,* or *porch monkey* didn't trigger mayhem, terror and death into the lives of Black African-American ancestors; instead, it was ONE word and *ONE* word only: n**ger.
The n-word is the most infamous and profane word in the English language. N**ger is the only slur in modern day terminology with an ignominious, malevolent and diabolical history. The origin, definition, and acts carried out under the guise of the term fueled the African-American Holocaust—a holocaust that, sadly, has been sanitized by American historians.

Non-blacks may be part of a group who is offended, insulted or angered when referred to as a *honky, cracker, hymie, kike, spic, spink, dago, wetback* to name a few; and not to justify use of the terms or detract from their offensiveness, the *only* common denominator between these words and the n-word is that they are all denigrating and demeaning slurs. Many assume that the n-word is no more than a racial slur, but none of the aforementioned slurs fit in the same context as the n-word. Non-black slurs are actually more comparable to terms such as the likes of *jigaboo, porch monkey, sambo, Uncle Tom, coon,* etc.

The n-word embodies actual events of enslaved Africans being kidnapped and transported from their own country; chained hand and foot onto a narrow ledge as the urine and feces from their fellow captives on the ledge above dripped down onto them; forced to endure inhumane conditions for three months as the slave ships transported them across the ocean. They then arrived in a country where they were to only witness and experience even further degradation and abasement.

Figure 1 Jesus Christ

With the first group of enslaved Africans being transported over on a vessel named the *"Good Ship Jesus"*, they unknowingly were being given a prelude to Americans using its Christian religion to justify their soon to be lives of hell and damnation. [3]

Even in knowing this hard and cold history, as seen in present day, the n-word is strung into every line of TV/movie scripts and hip-hop lyrics to make the entertainment more appealing and relatable to African Americans. Thanks to the marketing, globalization, and commercialization of the n-word; youths of all races now refer to one another as the n-word. In effect, Black America has given the entire world the green light to *trivialize* the dehumanization, butchering and slaughtering of their enslaved ancestors.

Rap artist NAS and wife at the 50ᵗʰ Annual Grammy Awards Feb. 2008

The *last* people on the face of this earth to even think about using the n-word should be the descendants of those who were truly victimized by this word. In fact, when descendants hear *anyone* use this term, it should send chards of glass shooting through their souls and disgust them to the point that they require the word be taboo in their presence no matter if the user is black or non-black.

The term n**ger, which defined enslaved Africans as 3/5 of a person, a sub-human, bestial savage beast that needed to be tamed, was not merely the result of slavery; it was the result of the distinct American form of enslavement known as chattel slavery. Unrestricted in his powers by institutions such as the State and the

Church, the American slave master had total control of his slave property. In a desire to maximize the profits of his investment, he strove to mold the *ideal* slave. This was achieved through continual unimaginable mental abuse, physical torment, severing of familial and cultural ties.

Subconsciously, the term n**ger/n**ga serves as a self-generating and self-refueling reinforced psychosomatic conduit to those who have been conditioned to accept its low vibratory rate of an all-consuming energy, conceivably, for an infinite period of time. An 18th century slave mentality is associated with use of the n-word:

An old woman, who was an escape slave, was once quoted in a conversation with a missionary as saying: "We are n**gers. We always was n**gers and we always shall be. We've got no souls. We's animals. We's black and so is the Evil One." The missionary protested: "The Bible doesn't say the devil is black." "Well," the old woman said, "White folks say so and we's bound to believe them, cause we's nothing but animals and n**gers. Yes, we's n**gers! N**gers! N**gers!"

As a slave, this old woman clearly had been conditioned and programmed to think of herself in such a manner. She may as well have been considered brain dead because she had been rendered incapable of thinking for herself. Even though she had escaped the physical rigors and bondage of slavery, the primary duty of *mental enslavement* had been accomplished. She still viewed herself as inferior to white people, sub-human and worthless; and because she spoke with great certainty and conviction about her identity, it is certain that she, and others with her same mindset, handed this image of poor self-worth down to future generations who carried this torch of shame well into their and their own descendants' futures.

Because of mind frames such as the old escape slave woman, this 18th century slave mentality is *still* alive and well. It consumes the hearts and minds of many 21st century Black African Americans who choose to waddle in a sea of ignorance as opposed to learning and thinking for themselves. Educated and uneducated alike share this affliction.

Unfortunately, the n-word is a surviving remnant of a psychological warfare that was waged to create dependency, and emotions, attitudes and/or behaviors to support achievement of a national objective—mental enslavement of a race of people. The *contemporary* Black African American users of the n-word validate this truth.

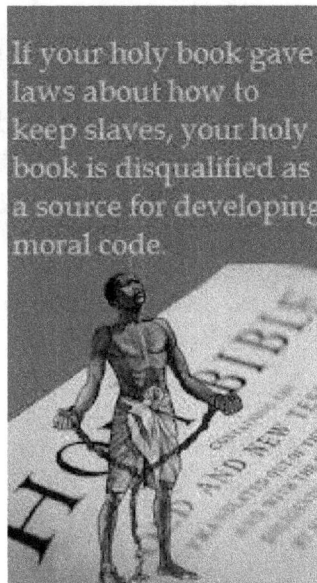

If your holy book gave laws about how to keep slaves, your holy book is disqualified as a source for developing moral code.

The term was used as an identifier and method of separating enslaved Africans from the remainder of the populous; it was used as a psychological conduit to breed thoughts of inferiority and, thus, no self-dignity, - pride, or –respect. The term was White America's way of refusing the enslaved as their equal, and accepting them as a so-called *white man's burden.* Because Africans were considered non-human, and, instead, animalistic, whites believed that in the eyesight of their Christian God, classifying the enslaved Africans as n**gers made it okay to dehumanize, brutalize and subject them to anything and everything ungodly. They further somehow conveniently justified that these acts of inhumanity were forgivable by God because they believed they were carrying out their God's work.

The Holy Bible was interpreted in many twisted ways to support White America's idea that black people were a cursed race and that God's word instructed them to "cleanse the world of impurities," which made it acceptable to enslave and dehumanize the subjugated Africans in efforts of fulfilling their God's will to make the world righteous again. Through the process of mind-bending and mental trickery, slave masters found it necessary to browbeat, brainwash and indoctrinate the African slaves into believing that they were indeed n**gers. Blacks were made to believe that whatever harm came to them was an act of God.

The n-word was one of the primary tools used in the adverse re-shaping of the African's psyche. Its continual use and acceptance in present day reiterates the image of the negative self-worth the word was meant to cultivate. Further, the negative self-appraisal is the key barrier necessary in restricting the individual's mind from reforming into a positive self-image.

Although many enslaved Africans sacrificed their lives

and fought hard to maintain the independent and healthy self-image they stood so firmly upon, the enslaved were eventually forced to perceive themselves as insignificant creatures through *physical, mental,* and *emotional coercion.* Over the past 400-plus years, much of Black America has suffered from this mental abuse, and continues to have difficulty realizing that their mind states are warped, misshapen, and need to once again be *changed* or *reformed* back to its natural state.

For more than 300 years, the n-word tag served as something more than a racial slur. The initial intent and purpose of the word served as a green light to terrorize, brutalize, maim, rape, kill, torture, castrate, sodomize with hot pokers, boil and burn alive a race of people who were considered to be lower than whale dung. Thus, any reference to someone as a "n**ger" served as a verbal reminder to their intellectual and physical status. It was a tool used to *mentally* enslave a race of people, *raping* and *abusing* their *minds* to accept an inferior image of themselves. The separation of classes— human versus n**ger—forced the subjugated to concretely assume an inferiority complex while simultaneously looking upon their slave masters as the superior and supreme race. To this very day, if some African Americans are asked why do they see themselves as the n-word, or a n**ga, their response will be because they are black and that all black folks are n**gahs.

N**ga/n**ger is an empty sign of self-hatred masquerading itself as a term of endearment. The idiom serves as perpetual imprisonment and is the detonator to the absolute extermination of an entire race of people's pride, dignity, honor and state of mind. Some may feel that the term carries no weight and plays no role in the current status and eventual outcome of the Black community. However, the term n**ga/n**ger was always meant to demean and destruct. Subsequently, as

African Americans continue to use the term, the community's ill-development will continue to occur. Words are a mighty source of power (Proverbs 23:7), and there is power—a negative, evil, conniving power—in giving life and use to the word "n**ga/n**ger."

The ravages of centuries of brutal mistreatment at the hands of whites through slavery, Jim Crow, segregation and lynch mobs still have a powerful psychological effect on black people to this very day. Today, when one hears African Americans using "n**ga" as part of their so-called private social vocabulary, it should be understood that they learned the word and its usage from the very institution whose intent and purpose was to not only enslave them physically but *mentally* as well. African Americans have yet to show that they have the strength to free themselves from the *mental* bondage of the n-word. Unable to handle the truth, they instead defer to irrational and lame excuses in allowing themselves to submissively surrender to a word that owns them in *heart, mind* and *soul.*

Contemporary Black America consigns to be *defined* by the very institution that dehumanized and enslaved their ancestry; they continue to accept a term drenched in ignorance, death, bloodshed, terror and carnage. A wise and liberated person knows that one never accepts someone else's definition of who they are—rather, liberated, self-aware individuals know that one *defines* themselves. (Note: Using the ghetto vernacular "n**ga" rather than "n**ger" does not qualify as a progressive "self-defining" term.)

Much confusion exists with both contemporary blacks and whites about the n-word. This confusion stems from a lack of knowledge about the historical meaning and intent behind the word. Even more importantly, they fail to understand that the n-word is more than just a word. A word that triggered and brought about death, bloodshed and terror into the lives of a group of people for more than three centuries is ungodly and obscene—and certainly more than *just* a word.

Many African Americans think and feel that mental enslavement no longer exists and/ or never did. They think the n-word is just a powerless term that has no effect or influence on any aspect of Black America. However, to this population of African Americans, one brings the question that if *mental* enslavement is not a problem, how do those who tolerate use of the n-word by black brothers and sisters come to this acceptance? How does their tolerance for use of the n-word serve as validation that they are a free and independent spirit? On the other hand, does use, acceptance, and/or tolerance of the n-word prove that this blinded population has been spoon fed by the powers to be to accept this categorization of their ancestors and self? How did they come to accept the idea that they are supposed to be a n**ga, and that being such a thing is okay? The history of the word n**ger cannot and should not be overlooked. The word is so stigmatized that to attempt to redefine it would suggest that an African-

American Holocaust never took place. The fact remains that an African-American Holocaust did occur, and no one—especially Black/African Americans—*should ever* take any action that detracts from or suggests any notion to the contrary.

Certainly, some words can change and evolve, and it may even be arguable that context can change certain words. However, other certain words saturated in a history of heinous, cruel acts and born from an original purpose/intent of breeding hatred, degradation, inferiority and mental genocide on a race of people cannot and will not *ever change* no matter its context or pronunciation of the term; n**ga/n**ger is such a word.

Once Black African Americans *acknowledge* that they have been mentally manipulated and *accept* that the n-word (n**ger/n**ga) is the lifeline that feeds the on-going systemic destruction, they will realize the importance of change.

Unfortunately, though, at this current juncture, most Black/African Americans have bought into the lie and the white man's image of the black man. African Americans need to address the lie to which they have so long allowed themselves to be a victim. They need to wake up to the deception that pervades their daily perceptions to finally embrace and present an image of who they are, what they truly were meant to be, and the grand people they can certainly attain. In so developing this paradigm, it will be clearly conveyed and understood that the true image of a Black African American is not that of a n**ger/n**ga.

To the contrary, the truest persona of the Black African American is the sharpest contrast to that of a n**ger. African Americans must come to realize that change *begins* within them—the vital key to self- empowerment

—and once they do so, the entire race will be able to move from ignorance, apathy and a veiled or false, destructive perspective of life to positive action.

Usage of the n-word and continual breeding of the 18th century *slave mentality* must stop. Use of the n-word serves a purpose, and that purpose never has been and never will be in the best interest of Black America. Some African Americans are totally convinced that the color of their skin is synonymous with the word n**ger. This ignorance must be rectified, and it can only be resolved collectively by Black Americans.

Since the word n**ger is as much a part of American history as slavery, the Civil War, and the Boston Tea Party, it would be naivety to assume that the word itself can be made to disappear—never to be seen, spoken or heard of again. If the word was completely erased from page and time, it would be equivalent to saying that the term's immoral history is some sort of illusion. Because the enslavement of Africans is just as an important piece in America's fabric as any other monumental historical event, one does not by any means expect for the term to be forever removed from the world's sight. However, the disparaging use of and reference to one another as the n-word can be rightly made to vanish or be abolished from the speech of all Black/African Americans *by* Black/African Americans, as it should be.

Thinking like helpless and hopeless victims, users of the word see a task such as eradicating use of the word as impossible. Such an attitude is the polar opposite of the prevailing boldness during the 1960's. In the '60's, the indomitable spirit of African Americans rejected references such as Negro and Colored, choosing, instead, to refer to themselves as Black/African American.

Rather than allowing White America to continue telling them who they were and how they would be viewed, African Americans of the '60's chose to define themselves based on their own principles of cultural dignity, value and appreciation. Just as that spirit of determination and striving toward self-respect and progress reigned throughout the '60's, Blacks of today can infuse that same spirit into *defining* themselves in a positive light rather than being *defined* by some past idea of inferiority. It is time to leave all remnants of the past in the past—including the n-word, and move forward with a clear head and self-definition founded on personal integrity, cultural and individual respect.

Racism

Racism is an unnatural demeanor invented by white people. Racism did not exist until the European enslavement of Africans. Racism is a power relationship between two groups. To be a racist, one group must have power and wealth to exact injustice upon another group.

Some will argue that the Nation of Islam's Minister Farrakhan is a racist but he *is not*; rather, as opposed to kowtowing, "going along just to get along," or being submissive to paternalism, he is *reacting* to unwarranted bigotry, oppression and racism. Farrakhan and no other African American are practicing racism because black people have not been able to come together to deprive or hurt another group; thus, individual blacks nor Black America are in a position to even begin to try to practice racism. Including the Black Panthers Party, it needs to be understood that their virulent rhetoric is a reaction *to* racism.

For more than five centuries, racism has legitimized assassinations, massacres and genocides. The doctrine of white supremacy has demonized, brutalized and dehumanized non-whites of the earth for centuries. Racism has been the global driving force behind the dispossession of continents, destruction of civilizations, and extermination of an entire people. [4]

Despite the long struggle against racism, it continues to pollute people's mental environment. Its enduring potency ensures that people are denied opportunities, justice and human rights. Key institutions remain racially monolithic. Racial privilege also endures as exampled by the Supreme Court's 2013 decision on the Voting Rights Act to allow nine states, mostly in the South, with a history of discriminating against minorities during voting time, to change their election laws without advance federal approval. This act alone validates the truth that racism still exist and is supported.

The 1638 Maryland Doctrine of Exclusion became, and still is in this 21st century, the doctrine of racism towards black people. As such, when African Americans "go along just to get along," accepting the notion that when they react to racism that the *reaction* itself can be construed as "reverse racism," is inaccurate and misleading and must *always* be rejected. [Note that, for clarity's sake, "reverse racism" in the above sentence is taken from White America's definition. This definition basically alludes to the idea that "reverse racism" occurs when those who typically experience racism, such as Black Americans, turn and thrust acts of racism upon those who are typically racist against them, such as White America. (At an even higher level, real intellects know that White America's definition of "reverse racism" is a copout and inevitable fear of what they see and feel as poetic justice. The enlightened ones know that White America's definition of reverse racism, to White America's relief, is implausible.)]

Other than the word n**ger, perhaps, the only other word in the English language that's as infamous and profane would be the term *racist*. The history between that's as infamous and profane would be the term *racist*. The history between these two words pretty much coincides like hand and glove. To unjustifiably call a white person a racist today is almost as bad as calling an African American a n**ger/n**ga. Both words remind each of an ugly untoward past and bring to light all of the negative feelings, struggle and strife experienced during a time of inequality, injustice, and inhumanity. It can be very injurious and hurtful to a white person to erroneously be labeled a racist as both *racist* and the n-word are volatile terms. Neither the n-word (n**ga) or the term racist should be used as loosely as both are today.

A bit of advice to non-blacks relative to those Black Americans who use the n-word: the Black community is divided on use of the insidious word n**ger/n**ga. As much as non-blacks may want to assist in helping cure this problematic use, understand that this is an issue that Black America is going to have to resolve for itself without any outside interference. Some non-blacks are genuinely concerned, but the last thing they need is to get caught up in cross-fires—complicating matters even further—attempting to mediate or intervene in a situation that requires Black/Africans Americans to resolve for themselves. Whether non-blacks are discouraging and/or encouraging African Americans about use of the n-word, they are better served by simply remaining silent spectators; it's a family matter that needs to be resolved without outside interference.

Some white people are making an even more egregious error of verbalizing the desire to use the n-word. They stand behind the foolish excuse that if blacks are using the term, why should the term be off limits to them? The larger question, though, is why are such whites fanning the flames of racism by voicing such an incendiary desire?

Two types of people use the n-word: racist people and those with an 18th century slave mentality. Respectable and honorable people, blacks and non-blacks alike, refrain from such usage. During the '60's, as the Civil Rights Movement took shape and began to gain traction with full force, African Americans no longer allowed themselves to be bullied into believing they deserved anything less than respect and equality. Thus, the phrase "Black is beautiful" became a rallying cry. Up until then, White America had associated being black to something undesirable, evil, and inferior. The stalwart spirit of the '60's was to *re-define* self and blackness as opposed to being *defined*. To some blacks and whites, any reference to Black History, Black American, African American, or Black Power is a form of racism; in actuality, however, these references are mere *reactions to* racism and tangible gifts of affirmation for, from, and to a people who refused to continue to be oppressed.

BLACK POWER

I'm an American, Not African-American

"A Man Without Culture Is Like a Zebra Without Stripes"
~African Proverb

There is no need for whites to use the term White History when essentially American and World History is just that in the guise of Euro-centricity teachings. By the time one graduates from college, they are well acquainted with Greek and Roman History (Western Civilization) which serves as a metaphor for white history. Therefore, any black student, unless they take it upon themselves to study Black History, will graduate from college totally illiterate of their *own* history. Many feel and think this is acceptable, just as they have been programmed and conditioned to.

America created a racial hierarchy with Whites at the top and Blacks at the bottom. Categorizing Blacks as n**gers justified the use of deceit, manipulation, and coercion to keep Blacks *in their so-called place* by any means necessary. Every major American societal institution offered legitimacy to the racial hierarchy and in this 21st century still do support this ideology. American and World History, which is presented to students in a prejudicial, sanitized and distorted manner, paints a picture of Blacks as inferior and Whites as superior. Only a *subservient* and *submissive* mind will tolerate such nonsense. Thus, once again, the American educational systemic supports the need for African studies as American and World History in general is racist and a glorified depiction of white superiority.

In a 1998 printing of the *Baltimore Sun* newspaper, Supreme Court Justice Clarence Thomas was quoted as saying: "Avoid that African-American studies stuff," adding that he will not hire a law clerk who has taken such courses. It's tragic that Clarence Thomas thinks so little of himself and the culture of his race. His evaluation of African American studies as "stuff" serves as a reflection of his Eurocentric indoctrination and cultural shame. Embracing one's heritage and culture is vitally important. It has everything to do with that person as an individual—no matter who they are or where they reside. Accepting one's culture is that unique separating factor that helps to ultimately enrich that person's life.

It is only Black African Americans who are in the dark about their roots. To deliberately remove self from one's heritage is the same as renouncing one's birthright and betraying their ancestors. Denying one's heritage would open an only makes room for a hole or gap in one's life that would likely be filled with superficial traditions that reflect nothing outside of self-denial. Clarence Thomas' transfiguration leaves him as the only non-European member sitting on the Supreme Court bench with a misguided Eurocentric mind and no real knowledge of self. To sit on the bench of the highest court in the land is a remarkable achievement, but not at the expense of selling one's soul and forfeiting one's own heritage. Clarence Thomas is an enigma, a question mark, a tool used with the only purpose of helping to maintain mind control of himself and his race.

Some African Americans are so alienated from their own culture and have become so Europeanized that any attempts by other Blacks to re-claim or talk about re-claiming their African culture is looked upon as being racist, bitter, or "stuck in the past." Outrageous! Every other group can lay claim to their culture without being considered any of the aforementioned, but the Black African American is considered such negative things if he chooses to pursue, honor, and recognize his own heritage.

Clearly, Blacks who make such claims have no interest in learning who they really are, and are comfortable with keeping lost their own identity and heritage while remaining enslaved to someone else's.

Moreover, these same African Americans are living proof of the effectiveness of the indoctrination process. Slaves were cut off from their roots and made to believe that their native culture and heritage was a shameful, primitive one filled with ignorance. Surprisingly, today's "educated" and ill-enlightened feel that any attempts to re-connect to their heritage is an act of racism or embarrassment. Either way, they remain disconnected from their very roots, and as such, are aliens amidst a crowd succumbing to systematic cultural assimilation policies, refusing to have their comfort zone disturbed.

I'm an American, *not* African American is often times an argument advanced by many of those lost ones who have chosen to walk in identity blindness, trying hard to fit in or align with a culture not their own. Hispanics have no problem identifying with their culture, Jewish people relate to their culture, Asians to theirs, Arabs to theirs, and so on. However, some Black Americans desire no part of identifying as an African descendant because they feel some sort of shame in being associated to Africans.

It matters not if one's Black heritage is linked to Haiti, Jamaica, West Indies, Caribbean, or India; ultimately, all roads somewhere down the line lead back to Africa, the Motherland. Everyone with a color-filled complexion has some connection to Africa; and if one chooses to learn of their past and origins, he/she will find that their truest history is indeed a remarkable marvel in which to be proud and one from which they should be more than thankful to have been born.

A positive identity to Africa has been removed from the minds of Black African Americans and replaced with the n-word image. This is a conspiracy that's working with the purpose of hoping Blacks will never, ever have the desire to rediscover the truth and learn of their great culture. Africa is the Cradle of Civilization. Black African Americans owe it to themselves and the precious memories of their ascendants to re-claim their rightful place in the chronicles of world history. They owe it to themselves to reject all things inferior especially the n-word categorization.

African Americans are the only people on the face of this earth who have been detached and separated from their ancient history and culture. Their acceptance of being defined as the n-word is not the mindset of a *free people*. Ironically, some black people will reject the notion of being referred to as an African but will embrace the n-word without hesitation, and will fight to defend their freedom of speech to use the word. Black record producer, Suge Knight validates the point when he recently in December 2013 on national television declared he is a n**ga and not an African.

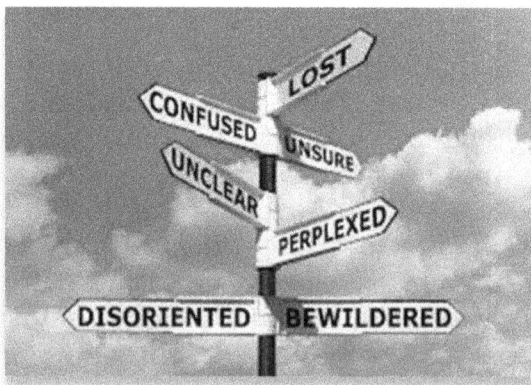

Many in the Black community share this sentiment of not referring to themselves as *African* Americans but simply as *Americans, Black Americans* or more succinctly a n**ga. They do this in efforts to highlight the fact that they are natural-born American citizens and/or to detach themselves from the African culture. However, a dilemma of sorts exists in this context considering white Americans do not refer to themselves as *White* Americans or *Euro-Americans*—but then again, do they need to refer to themselves as such? Each and every white American knows and identifies with their culture be it German, Dutch, Scandinavian, British, French, and so forth. The same cannot be said for Black African Americans, many of whom have been conditioned to be in denial and resentful of their African heritage.

Is it racist to refer to self as "African American" or even to celebrate Kwanzaa? Some see the celebration of Kwanzaa as a racist act. Some propose that Blacks should view themselves as Americans rather than African Americans, and, thus, should have no separate holiday. Some promote rejecting the holiday completely, using the justification that Blacks would protest a white racist if they created a holiday to celebrate whiteness.

Perhaps, people should conduct their due diligence and research the origin of Christmas, Easter, Halloween, and even the Christian religion itself which serves as an advocacy platform for white supremacy. Ironically, the ethnocentrism celebrations of Cinco de Mayo (Hispanic and Latino), as well as Rosh Hashana, Yom Kippur, and Chanukah, just a few of the numerous Jewish holidays, are not considered racism. However, any attempt by Black African Americans to introduce, acknowledge or celebrate any form of African culture is considered racist, taboo, or shameful. Black African Americans need to stop living within the confined boundaries of the 400-year-old anesthesia and start paying attention.

Moreover, even if the above-mentioned holidays are considered "real," the fallacy in the thinking of those who oppose "newly-created" African American holidays is that one must understand that the existing holidays were also "new" at some point in time; it's just that they have been widely accepted and acknowledged for so long and are so strongly ingrained in American culture that no one ever questions the relevance or purpose behind those holidays. Instead, everyone blindly joins in the tradition of celebration.

On another note, whites and other races who felt their beliefs, culture, and heritage were significant and must be shared with the world did their work centuries ago to ensure their importance would always be acknowledged. In present time, they have no need to create new holidays to bring awareness and honor to their beliefs, traditions, or history. These ideologies are already heavily incorporated into virtually *all* Americans' daily lives and culture.

The enslaved and their descendants have been led to believe that African Americans have no worthwhile past and that the Black race has done nothing significant since the beginning of time. They have been programmed to accept that anything black is inferior or evil and anything white is superior or pure. What has been said of African Americans during the past four centuries has been mainly for the purpose of cultivating a particular inferior mind state to keep them in this substandard place of living—psychologically and socially. It has been so effective that many Blacks reside in "that place" to this very day, always saying, "[t]his is just the way it is—has always been and will be." What is more is that the African American community has continued to pass along this falsehood—along with many others—from generation to generation.

The entire institutionalized American system is based on Eurocentric values, principles and philosophies. That, truly, in itself is racist. The city school systems, colleges, universities and the media are not going to provide the kind of information that will help build the self-esteem of a black student. No traditional system in America is going to support and facilitate an information stream that will free and release one's mind from prevailing Eurocentric intellectual mentalities to the unabridged truth. This is a racist mentality-enslaving agenda!

As a consequence, many mentally enslaved Blacks become a ventriloquist for white supremacy. They view any efforts to restore black culture as being racist. They are in a state of denial which is symptomatic of being mentally enslaved. Such mentality is an illness that is generally defined as abnormal. The abnormalities in these instances are based on two variables: 1) acceptance and behavior patterns that reflect a belief that a European value system is superior; and 2) a negative outlook and shame on anything promoted as Black or African American.

These ventriloquists/sycophants also view the efforts to restore Black culture as a way to promote separatism and/or oppress White America. However, this is not the case. The point is to bring Black Americans up to par on their culture and history so that they have a true foundation to which to cling and build self-awareness. The reason so many Blacks feel alienated or a non-fit in America is because they are attempting to attach their black roots to a white foundation. *This can never work—* it is a recipe for being utilized as a manipulative tool by another race, while also remaining a lost, drifting spirit seeking something they will never be able to attain or grasp.

Much can be said for an ideal utopian America where all

are treated equally and given fair opportunity. However, a leveled playing field must be established first. In order for one to reach that equal ground, which is built upon total and complete self-acceptance and -awareness, he/she must become cocooned, immersed, saturated in his/her ethnic and cultural heritage/history. In so doing, Black America will find their greatest connection to this life; they will feel *found* and no longer wandering aimlessly in a land not politically or socially built for their survival.

Black/African Americans must realize that they are not Europeans! Yes, it is acceptable to understand the European history as it strongly integrates with the African and African-American history; however, this does not make one a member of the European race. Once Black America *first* understands its own history, *then* how it intermingles with other races' histories, the community will be able to remove the false veil from its covered eyes to see a world in which all of the opportunity, pitfalls, and truest realities are made clear.

Only then can one understand their true plight or purpose in this life and take flight in that positive direction to productively contribute to a unified society. As well, by understanding one's heritage and history, one is better able to sympathize with the unfortunates of their race and devise ways to help enlighten these people to become empowered, self-sufficient citizens.

White America has never lost touch with their European values and principles. They know who they are and do not discount where their heritage lies, dating back to ancient Greece and Rome. Blacks, on the other hand, have a very rich and cultivated heritage but refuse to acknowledge, in many cases, that their roots are African. By denouncing African roots, one is unknowingly advocating the once force-fed acceptance of European traditions, slavery, and disorientation of the Black American. Because of this, many Blacks remain non-self-aware, lost souls or ventriloquists for another's plight.

Consider the fact that other than the Black African American, no other race of people are inclined to abandon their culture in an attempt to adopt and integrate into a Eurocentric culture. It is time for African Americans to awaken from the 400-year-old anesthesia to which they have been subjected, and recognize the abnormalities in their behavior.

Acknowledging Kwanzaa would be one of the right steps to take in helping Black African Americans re-establish their identities—unless of course Blacks choose to remain ashamed of being black as the indoctrination process was set in place to accomplish. Thriving Black civilizations maintain dates of existence to well before the Aztecs, Mayans, Greeks and Romans. High time has come for Black America to take back the strong cultural identity that was stolen and contorted into some dishonorable, foul, worthless sense of being. Black America must stop acting victimized and no longer remain powerless to an on-going 400-year-old mind control game.

Some may have a problem with Kwanzaa's founder Dr. Maulana "Ron" Karenga and, perhaps, these concerns do not go unfounded. However, one should not lose the spirit, meaning, and intent of the holiday based on popular opinion of its founder. Kwanzaa, which represents all of Africa as a Pan-African holiday, celebrates family and community. Kwanzaa is based on the seven principles that promote togetherness and establish a foundation of societal progress; these principles include unity, self-determination, collective work and responsibility, collective economics, purpose, creativity, and faith.

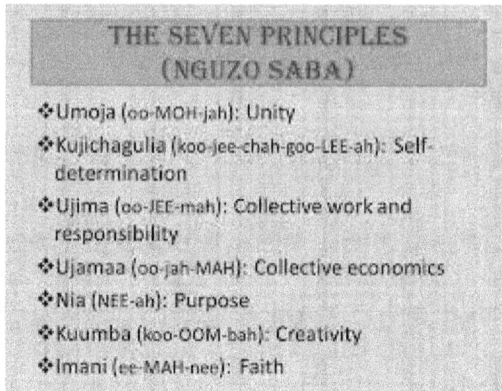

THE SEVEN PRINCIPLES
(NGUZO SABA)

- Umoja (oo-MOH-jah): Unity
- Kujichagulia (koo-jee-chah-goo-LEE-ah): Self-determination
- Ujima (oo-JEE-mah): Collective work and responsibility
- Ujamaa (oo-jah-MAH): Collective economics
- Nia (NEE-ah): Purpose
- Kuumba (koo-OOM-bah): Creativity
- Imani (ee-MAH-nee): Faith

As well, before one chooses to immediately cast away any credibility in the holiday and founder, lest not forget that America itself initially consisted of England's undesirables, crooks, murderers and thieves; they were shipped to America because there was no hope of their rehabilitation. Now, America is the greatest country on earth, many thanks of course to the sweat, blood and tears of African enslaved ancestors.

The founder of Kwanzaa, whose past is somewhat soiled and tainted, should not interfere with recognizing and acknowledging the positive aspects of Kwanzaa and what it brings to the African-American community. Kwanzaa serves as a step in the direction of unification, and that for many non-blacks is cause for concern. Any attempt by Black America at unification is going to always be met with strong resistance. African Americans must not jump on the train of continual sabotage; rather, they must find the good in efforts such as Kwanzaa to use as a tool in re-gaining the much-needed collective self-awareness.

Many opponents of Kwanzaa reject the holiday and question its significance, but will openly accept and embrace the n-word without question—even while well-

knowing the history of the n-word. How preposterous is that? A word connected to the mutilating, butchering and slaughtering of countless millions of African American ancestors is used with no end by their descendants.

Regardless to its newness or past life of its founder, for the liberated mind, accepting Kwanzaa as a "real" holiday should be a no-brainer. Embracing Kwanzaa would be realized as a step in the direction of American-born Blacks finally embracing their ancestry and that their realest history lies in a rich African heritage. By accepting this truth and living fully in its rays, black unity, liberation, and progression can become a reality.

Chapter 3

Betrayal of African Forefathers

"You can't have a positive life with a negative mind"
~African Proverb

Freedom riders of the '60's Civil Rights Movement stood firmly and proudly upon the legacy of their forefathers. They gave every bit of themselves to ensure future generations had an even firmer foundation upon which to not only establish economic success but, most importantly, to re-claim and bring back to the forefront the need and demanding of self- and cultural respect within and without the Black community.

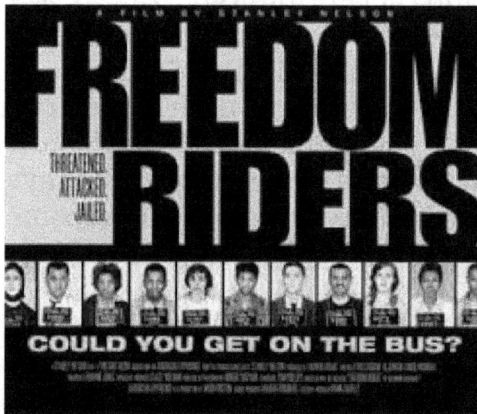

During this period, a fed up group of people began to establish their own healthy self-images and associate self-respecting terms to themselves, which included the birth of the term *African American*. They rejected such terms as *Colored* and *Negro*, because they desired strongly to define themselves as opposed to being defined. Any negative associations to the past were pushed into the background, which allowed the spotlight to shine upon black power, black progress, and the opening of the flood gates to re-build a positive, unified, prosperous, and self-respecting Black America.

But then, something happened. Possibly, Black America became too opportunistic, too arrogant at the first few major advances accomplished; or too free before *real* freedom was actually attained. Black America was only given a small slather, taste, or an "inch"...and with this small ration being far more than past portions, Black America ran with it, not realizing how much more was left to be gained nor how much had been sacrificed. It is as if Black America forgot how much was endured to attain this level and just chose to live in the moment— with the community being somewhat fixed and somewhat broken, never reaching a collective unity and direction.

Then again, in retrospect, it may not have been anything remotely connected to the aforementioned speculations but just simply a lack of a *real* plan on how to proceed or maybe it was the unsuspecting ramifications of integration and/or a combination of both.

Nonetheless, in order for African Americans to rise above their *current state* of complacency and reach their promise—as an initial step—all community members, regardless of status and background, must consider the task at hand—burying the n-word—a serious issue, one of highest priority, and commit to exonerating the demeaning expression from all vocabulary banks.

The contemporary Black African Americans steadfastly refuse to hold one another *accountable* for their own actions, and believe that the n-word and its focus is less tailored or relevant to today's societal. This notion could not be further from the truth; nonetheless, for illustration purposes, if that is indeed the case, then simply out of respect for the struggles and sacrifices of their forefathers, it should be considered an abomination for any person of color to embrace the n-word.

These same people continually devise some asinine justification to support use of the n-word. A few of the "justifications" allude to the idea that Black users of the word are taking the sting out of the term or reversing its power by using it themselves. Some say they are changing the meaning of the idiom by using it endearingly and changing the suffix on the word from "er" to "a". Any person with sense knows that the word "n**ga" cannot exist without "n**ger" as the ghetto vernacular of the term is simply a variation of the real term. If two branches are connected to the same tree, it's a safe bet they share the same roots. The N-word is the *ultimate expression* of white supremacy and racism, irrespective of the way it is pronounced or spelled.

Further, users of the idiom believe that its relevance is no longer substantial and only encompasses Black African Americans' ascendants and all the hell they caught as a result of being categorized as such. These users say that those who fight against the term's use live in the past and are unable to let go of it. The truth of the matter is those proponents of the term will go to any length to cover up their act of ignorance for their use of the vile word. Their justifications for use of the term shows that they are either indifferent or in *denial* about all that occurred relative to the sinister baggage that comes along with this word.

If any argument can be made, it should be that proponents of the term are mentally incapacitated and too inertia to overcome their use of it. To be clear, accepting use, remaining indifferent to its use, or using the n-word is the same as sanctioning all that transpired against the black ancestry. The n-word is so *saturated with filth, so polluted* with the ruling class stereotypes, that the only reasonable alternative is to euthanize it.

If the term carries no weight in present day, then why do some Blacks go so far as to say that it is okay or acceptable for Blacks to use the n-word and unacceptable for non-blacks to use it? Worthy to note: some white folks may play along with the silly game, knowing that with or without some so-called permission they are going to use the term, anyway, if they have a mind to do so. Blacks naively--by setting the wrong examples—encourage whites and other non-blacks to use the term through their own use of it in daily interactions, music lyrics and other forms of entertainment.

Any self-respecting Black African American who is proud of him/herself and their ancestry is incapable of identifying as a n**ga/n**ger. These dignified individuals would become appalled—almost if not certainly—to the point of physical contest if anyone referred to them as such. This type of enlightened person has transcended the inferior state of mind, and now, instead, owns the rightful higher perception of self. This self-respecting person toys with no one who approaches them at any other affirmed level of understanding. On the other hand, a *mentally enslaved* individual lies fully relaxed and engulfed, or maybe even indifferent, in the idea of being a n**ger/n**ga, and finds it humorous and acceptable to encourage others to the same. The pejorative term served and still does serve as a determination to deny human status to certain people.

If someone was to create a situation comedy based on the actions of African Americans and their use of the n-word, it would make the all-time ding-a-ling list. This is because of the walking contradiction Black America on the whole seems to be when it comes to use of the n-word. Ultimately, African Americans must stop being so concerned about the dealings and references to Black America occurring outside of Black America, and really *focus* in on what Black America *feels* about its own community and unified self.

Think of it this way: when a competitor hits the track, football field, or basket-ball court, that athlete cannot be concerned about what the opponent or the competing crowd says about them; rather, that athlete just has self and the belief he/she has about his/her capabilities, which is that person's only solace. That athlete must perform, even with the world against them, to the best of their ability to reach the level of success they seek in spite of the negativity swirling about. Instead of wasting their energy or becoming distracted on the crowd, the athlete must go into self to prove to self and the world the greatness of which he/she is made. Once that athlete attains that level of success—wins the game or race by a long shot, the opponent and competing crowd have no choice but to close their rioting mouths and pay respect where it is due.

This is the same position Black America must take. In order to re-build itself, Black America must stop worrying so much about what is going on outside the community and re-claim the dignity within first. Once the African American community is re-established as a self-respecting race of people who only refers to self in honorable and respectable terms, the rest of the world *will have no choice* but to do the same. Black America will also no longer have to worry about being this "walking contradiction" and policing use of the n-word. Still, this process of "winning" begins with what African Americans think of self.

This is the 21st century, but yet, racism still exists, and it seems as though Black African-American proponents of the n-word insist on feeding the flames of racism by promoting, marketing and commercializing the term. Proponents of the n-word say that people give words power. These same proponents believe that they have taken a hateful word and turned it into a positive, removing the sting from the idiom by boastfully referring to one another as the n-word and using it as a term of endearment.

Truth be told, though, their use of the n-word keeps the hate, inferior/superior mindset complex, inequality, and racial disrespect at the forefront of everyone's minds, consciously or sub-consciously. The word is a slave-oriented epithet imposed on Americans of African descent by slave masters. It is a grotesque conception of Black African Americans which has been shaped in the Eurocentric mind and forced with Procrustean cruelty on the person and personality of African Americans.

Circling back to a few previous points made: if only black people are supposed to use the word n**ga and are doing so in order to accomplish a transference of power or to prove that the term no longer has a racially-offensive connotation, the attempt has proven futile because the term is still taboo if used by other races in reference to black people. White people, for instance, still cannot say the word n**ger without inviting some sort of hostile reaction. If Blacks have truly successfully revolutionized and taken the sting out of the word, then everyone—black and non-black—would be free to use the word without question of racism, socioeconomic class, or the context in which the term was used.

Moreover, although the word is claimed as an endearing term when used among Blacks, as soon as one falls into a fit of anger, the word becomes an instrument of hate. This is an oxymoron because if African Americans have taken the "sting" out of the word, how can they turn around and use it to, well, spew out venomous hatred towards another black person? This is the type of ridiculousness and insanity that exists in the Black community, and it seems many African Americans are okay with such conflicting behavior just as they have been programmed to accept.

Other than the African-American user of the n-word, the rest of the world plainly recognizes and sees that word for its inherent intent. The n-word suggests that black people are second class citizens, ignorant and less than human. The n-word is a term of exclusion and verbal justification for discrimination and violence. It matters not how the n-word is spelled or pronounced—the same as brother/brotha, sister/sista, sucker/sucka, etc. Use of the word n**ga is ghetto vernacular for n**ger, and ultimately, its purpose and intent will always be the same. The idiom serves as a psychological conduit that negatively manipulates and shapes the minds and collective perceptions of America's black population to perceiving an unfavorable and false perception of self.

The term will always stand for what it represented. No matter how one says it, the idiom will always and forever spew of African forefathers' unrighteous-shed blood, stolen innocence of helpless children, and sorrowful, inconsolable cries of childless mothers.

Incredibly, some African Americans search for pseudo-intellectual reasons to refer to themselves as n**gahs, as opposed to discovering authentic reasons to self-negate away from the term. Perhaps, this is because media only greatly promotes/targets seekers of pseudo-intellectual reasoning—selling them on superficial delights and something that "sounds good," as opposed to targeting the effective populous, which includes those with alternative thinking or real intellect. The pseudo-intellects seek or accept just enough "knowledge" to make them seem well-informed or as if they are in control of their own decisions but still comfortable enough to fit within the status quo of indifference. This fence-straddling position is a common ground of belief where use of the n-word should not be censored.

Unless an individual has the mental resolve and intestinal fortitude to expose how Black history in general is being sanitized and censored, they should smartly refrain from speaking about how the n-word should not be censored or sanitized. Anything less, that person is completely out of order and is allowing self to be used as a tool, pawn, or puppet to maintain the status quo.

At some point, Black America must come to grips with itself and stop allowing the community to be hoodwinked and bamboozled by a systemic harboring a cryptic agenda. The Paula Deen's of America serve as a perfect example of this phenomenon: the news media aroused the entire country against her because of her use of the n-word. The only supposed power this woman has is the power to insult; other than that, she and others like her have no power, which is why they attempt to degrade others to make themselves feel worthy. Yet, it is folks like Deen who whenever they make a misstep and use the n-word, the necessarily-required attention is never directly cast upon the ugliness of the term.

No real focus is put on the true ramifications the term manifests on the progress of generations of black youth, nor to the implications upon the mal-progression of the American psyche as it relates to black people. Instead, all of the attention is drawn toward that person, and how their actions will now affect their pocketbooks.

This action draws attention away from the institutions who are the real culprits with enormous power to manipulate, oppress and control. These institutions will of the n-word; rather, they publicize all use of the n-word and just simply treat black people like one. Their primary objective is to maintain a national objective that's never been abandoned, further perpetuating a mental exploitation and suppression of an unsuspecting group of people.

N**ger is an inferior category and place reserved for those African Americans who are gullible enough to accept the term. During slavery, enslaved blacks had no choice but to accept such categorization; today, their descendants have a choice but are timid about leaving their comfort zone, their pre-appointed place of being n**gers. So, what do they do? They dupe themselves into accepting the ghetto vernacular (n**ga) as some nonsensical term of endearment. That action in itself basically safeguards White America's plight of destruction against the Black community at the Black community's own hand.

Embracing the n-word serves as a sanctioning of every whip lash and evil perpetuated upon Black African Americans' beloved ancestry. This is not a consensus or opinion; it is a fact. Deliberate or not, it is sanctioning nonetheless, and such behavior is neither magnanimous nor altruistic. No. It is indeed the opposite—malevolent, mean-spirited, self-centered and narrow-minded. Black ancestors deserve better in the perspective of reverence and honor of their sacred and hallow memories. The n-word should be taboo and forbidden to be a part of the Black African American culture and lexicon.

Many African American users of the term fail to realize that there is nothing cute, chic or cool about the word n**ger/n**ga. They must open their eyes to the fact that though the evil events took place decades ago, it was their very own ancestors who were victimized. Out of respect and a sense of decency, Black America must stop making a mockery of their ascendants sacred memories, hardships, struggles and sacrifices by embracing a word that dehumanized, terrorized, and caused bloodshed and death into the lives of so many innocent people.

If somehow the context of history can be changed to obliterate the wrongs committed against people; restore life to the murdered, honor to the dishonored, property to those who have been wronged; *and force the scales of human and divine justice to recover their equilibrium,* then and only then perhaps an embrace of the n-word would be condoned. In such situation, the term would not be covered in such heart-ache, destruction, cultural and mental genocide. However, at this current juncture, the term is still drenched in the ugliness in which it was originally intended.

Embracing and accepting this word implies condoning all the sordid acts that were executed by those who brutally raped black women and all the rest of the fiendish, sadistic, vicious and bloodthirsty acts perpetrated upon African-American ascendants. Their memories should always be held sacred and canonized. If a person has any ounce of self-worth or respect, they will no longer be browbeaten into accepting the notion that the n-word is just a meaningless word.

African Americans can do better than this! Each and every time they laughingly invoke use of the n-word or condone use of it, that action serves as a testimony to the ungratefulness, self-serving, small-minded and mean-spiritedness that still lives. Blacks *demand* respect from White America, but dismisses any ultimatums for *self*-respect. Something is terribly wrong with this picture and *only* Black America can correct it, not White America.

Nothing empowering exists in embracing the n-word; it has no benefit or value. Continually holding on to the name given Blacks by a racist society through using, defending and supporting the use of the word, as well as trying to rationalize that it has been changed into something positive, is sheer insanity. African Americans' defiant use of the incorrigible, demonic and evil n-word is an abomination to the canonized, sacred and hallowed memories of those who were dehumanized and subjected to menticidal conditions. The sacrifices, ordeals and struggles of their ancestors must not and should not be taken lightly. If so, a heavy price will and is being extracted for such negligence.

Time has come that the Black community develop some backbone and emancipate their own minds from the tyrant word n**ga. No other race or culture can, nor should they try, to accomplish this feat for Black America; and quite frankly, the African American community does not need anyone else to correct this problem. As every man must fight his own battles in life to succeed, so it is the Black community's responsibility to take up its load and strive for their freedom and self-respect—from within and without the community.

The newly-enlightened will elect genuine thoughts of truth that allow real freedom of thought, raising the mind power, over the contaminating false truth they have known for so long. The n-word is an evil word that sanctioned the destruction of tens of millions of Black ascendants over a 300-plus-year African-American Holocaust, and continues to shackle the Black community today.

Each person must re-shape their mind and recognize that word for what it is so that they can effectively reform their realities and assist in returning Africa America to a proud, self-respecting, unified and progressive group of people. This will help raise the standards of the community to newer and greater heights.

Although *not* all African Americans refer to themselves as the pejorative n-word, an alarming proportion of the Black community uses and/or supports use of the term. For instance, ministers invoke the word from their pulpits, and the NAACP, with the wink of the eye, looks the other way when prominent Blacks publicly embrace the word. This response serves as an unwritten law or sentiment within the Black community that says, "Thou shall not speak ill of another Black." The approach is that dirty laundry should not be aired out publicly, which makes sense and is understandable only if the point being made is to benefit the entire Black race.

Some may also refrain from speaking on others' use of the term, thinking that if they say nothing about it—just ignore use of the term, that everyone else will as well. However, if issues detrimental to the over-all well-being of the community continue to be swept under the rug or ignored, the only alternative is to bring awareness to the issue and make it public so that the concern does not perpetually go unabated.

Many black college professors support and encourage their students' use of the word. It is liberally promoted in mainstream media, such as in the music of rappers, Hollywood and television shows like *The Boondocks*. In grassroots Black America, many are simply so consumed by the word, that they are unable to survive a 24-hour period without invoking the term.

To be candid, Blacks who refrain from the use of the word are *not* in denial of the 300-year African-American Holocaust. Acknowledging the sinister history of the n-word is not giving power to the word as some claim. However, accepting use of the word does subliminally give it power even though one does not realize it at the surface level; when one is referred to as a "n**ga", all of the memories of contempt, negativity and inferiority courses through one's veins and mental. Just think

To be candid, Blacks who refrain from the use of the word are *not* in denial of the 300-year African-American Holocaust. Acknowledging the sinister history of the n-word is not giving power to the word as some claim. However, accepting use of the word does subliminally give it power even though one does not realize it at the surface level; when one is referred to as a "n**ga", all of the memories of contempt, negativity and inferiority courses through one's veins and mental. Just think about it: for almost four centuries, some very heinous and terrible atrocities occurred to Black African Americans' beloved ancestors in the name of the n-word. It was a term of exclusion and verbal justification for inhumane acts to be carried out against African Americans, including slaughtering, butchering, brutal rapings, death and unwarranted terrorizing.

For an individual to adopt n**ga as a term of endearment, that person is either in a continued state of denial or the word has subconsciously over-powered and brainwashed that individual into his/her so-called "place." Either way, acceptance and use of the term has caused the progress and rejuvenation of the Black community to remain stagnant and the demise to continue.

The rationales for self-internalization of the n-word are many. One of the more interesting ones centers on the infringement of freedom of speech. However, considering the contradictory manner in how the n-word is used, such comments are nothing more than an insult to a thinking person's intelligence. In response to the freedom of speech concern, other than the African American, no one argues about protecting their rights to demean and degrade themselves except for those with shackled minds. Also, with freedom of speech comes accountability and responsibility for one's actions. Try yelling *fire* or *bomb* in a public place filled with people and see what the consequences will be.

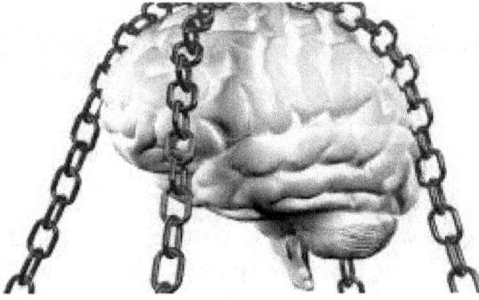

Presently, no on-going annual events acknowledging and exalting the strength, courage, fortitude and resilience of the African American's stalwart ascendants' abilities to survive the horrific calamities they endured are put to record. Without their tenacity to survive, no African-American descendant would be here today. Use of the n-word is tantamount to Black Americans spitting on their ancestors' graves, sanctioning every whip lash, rape, disemboweling, castration, hanging, and torture that was performed on them.

Out of shame of being identified as descendants of slaves, many Blacks tend to distance themselves from all that occurred during the African-American Holocaust, with the exception of the uncontrollable 18th century slave mentality use of the n-word. These Blacks really have no idea who they are or own any knowledge of the long-line of their proud, strong heritage and ancestry before the days of oppression.

Each time Blacks call one another n**ga or n**ger as terms of so-called endearment, the memories and spirits of the Black forefathers are desecrated and dishonored, ignoring their history and the great pains and struggles they suffered in America. Duty is calling and the time is now for *all* Blacks to bestow upon ancestors a better and more dignified place in the Black race's collective memory than any individual money-hungry rapper, self-centered comedian, or blind revisionist has accorded them to date. It is current day African-Americans' duty and call to accord their ancestors a better place in the race's collective memory.

Concerned African Americans must continue to follow-up and relentlessly help work toward changing the thinking of the Black community—the young and the old, and drive them to more positive and noble pursuits. The Black community must share the serum of healthy self-respect with others most in need of hope. The community can have tremendous impact and become that agent of change. However, the collective Black community must first believe it has the ability to make the change, and take strides at every level to re-program the Black community's psyche to restore the dignity, respect, and cultural pride that once illuminated the very essence of the Black race.

Chapter 4

Rap Artists' and Entertainers' Use of the N-word (N**ga)

"When there is no enemy within...the enemies outside can't hurt you."
~African Proverb

Fifty years removed from 1964, and the state of affairs throughout the Black community is on life support. Black-on-Black crime, gangs, rampant drug selling and addictions; a high volume of incarcerations, probations, paroles; and problems in schools such as suspensions, expulsions and poor performances are not just externally caused conditions. In fact, the primary causes of these concerns stem from internal influences within the Black community as well.

Due to a leadership void left unfilled for too long, the African American community sought a familiar voice that shared their same woes and sentiments. The spotlight that was once filled with the likes of Martin Luther King, Jr. and Malcom X during the '60's was now being shined upon the hip-hop movement. Depleted words of solace, hope, and constructive activism were replenished with powerful rap lyrics of frustration, degradation, and instant self-gratification. In the mid-80's, a rap group called N.W.A., acronym for *N***az With Attitude*, popularized gangsta rap to become pied pipers for a leaderless generation.

They promoted misogyny, violence, a gangsta way of life, and anything and everything that construed a debased way of living. As a result, the hearts and minds of a generation of children were affected in a negative way. Many learned to see no value in having a strong work ethic or acquiring knowledge and morality; this mentality eventually led to the imprisonment of an increased number of young African-American males who, in some twisted fashion, treat incarceration as some sort of badge of honor or rites of passage. Their viewing jail or prison as a necessary step in becoming a man is perhaps a metaphor for feelings of a victimized and hopeless attitude.

In today's contemporary times, it seems almost as if the n-word is just simply another racial slur or derogatory word. However, it is not the supposed contemporary definition of the word that is so controversial; rather, it is the historical baggage that comes along with and cannot be separated from the word regardless to the time in human history, present or future at which the term is being used. Though the context of a word can change, the context of the n-word's immutable history cannot be changed. The only way the term could potentially be changed is if the African-American Holocaust can somehow be erased by undoing all the countless millions of tragic killings, brutal rapes, inhumane mutilations, and the deliberated and systematic destruction of a group's mind.

The senseless rebuttals that are advanced by proponents of the n-word are that it is just a word, there are more important things to worry about, and that the word has been taken back and redefined. These mentally and emotionally scarred descendants of slavery are so severely disturbed psychologically that they actually believe that they can change the meaning of this particular word. More importantly, though, considering the term's immoral, evil and ugly background, *why* would anyone even want to try to re-claim or change its meaning? With a thing so ugly, why would one want to even "see" it still living?

For decades, the African-American's consciousness has been submerged in a toiling, never-ending sea of self-

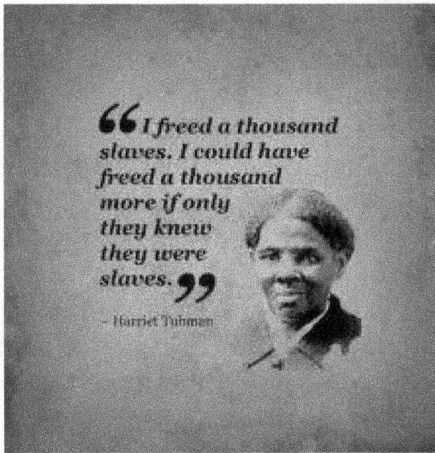

&& I freed a thousand slaves. I could have freed a thousand more if only they knew they were slaves. 99

– Harriet Tubman

deprivation, and ultimately, self-destruction, at their own discretion. The minds of its youths were and are exposed to the poison and venomous lyrics of rap music and the Stepin Fetchit antics of black comedians. The argument that's advanced is that these rap artists are poets painting a picture of how life is in the Black community and that they should have complete autonomy with freedom of expression. This logic is analogous to saying since strychnine looks like sugar, it must be sugar, so just feed everyone strychnine. Simply put, what looks like gold is not always gold. The antics of rap artists are mental poison.

Another point to make is just because black rappers do certainly have the right to speak about their lives in their lyrics, it is not impossible to convey one's point with great, powerful expression and still respect the memories of Black ancestors. Moreover, rappers' and entertainers' inability to strike a chord in their audiences without use of the n-word or their intellect to find other words to still strongly convey their message speaks to their ill-education and proves that their parents, too, were conduits and guilty of mental enslavement...

Such acceptance and promotion of the glorification of

violence, sex, drugs, and profanity as a lifestyle leads to an unhealthy, broken and unproductive environment. This same acceptance and rationalizing with defiling behaviors and attitudes serves as a breeding ground for trouble, despair, discord, discontent and afflictions of grave consequences.

The explosion of Black violence, glorification of the "gangsta" image in film and song, and enshrining of black male toughness continually paint a grim picture of Black self-destruction. It types young black males, especially if hooded, as a mortal threat to society. This pictorialization serves as a direct assault of the Black image on the international stage and under no circumstances benefits Black African Americans.

This is not to say that hip-hop culture is the sole cause of ills presently enveloping the Black community; however, unfortunately, the culture in many ways cultivates and contributes to the self-mutilating behaviors, attitudes and lifestyles of the Black African-American community. The image presented to the world is very unhealthy and disconcerting; the stage portrayal of the Black community seems almost as if black folks are being set up to self-destruct. The encouragement of self-destructive behavior and attitudes must be abated not to alleviate the perception, but to re-create real upstanding black people.

When one listens closely to the lyrics of rap music, the n-word is used and embraced in the same context with guns, a criminal lifestyle, drugs, and denigration of women. All of these factors are an advocacy of a self-destructive culture. Such negative imagery is reminiscent of methods used in the chattel slavery era to emasculate the minds of the enslaved—except in these modern times, mental enslavement is conducted in a more creative way at the hand of the African American in conjunction with exploitative corporate executives.

Hip-Hop music is an art form all unto itself. Its unique rhythmic beat and craftily-packaged rhymes can be very catchy, entertaining and stimulating. Because listeners are often caught up by the beat and impressed with the artist's literary creativity, and, perhaps are just happy to see one of their own finally make it, they tend to overlook and/or downplay the real message(s) being conveyed. This may help to explain why some rap records with self-destructive, violent, demeaning and insensitive lyrics in nature can be so popular. Perhaps, rappers feel that they are just entertaining storytellers, saying what "sounds good," but the truth of the matter is that their messages do carry clout, are influential, and can evoke action. As such, they must be mindful of what they say; moreover, the artists and their sponsors must be held accountable for the artists' actions and words.

Hip-hop's promotion and marketing of the n-word in context with drugs, crime, violence, denigration of black women, and the unrelenting daily assault on the Black psyche is designed to maintain and adversely shape the minds and collective consciousness of America's black population.

When Black/African Americans support rappers and entertainers that humiliate and degrade their own race, those supporters are participating in cultural, mental genocide and the sanctioning of every whiplash and other atrocities felt by enslaved ancestors. These same fans are contributing to the emotional, psychological, spiritual, and cultural extermination of the Black race as the entire world watches in amazement at such abnormal behavior.

During the mid-90s, Michael Jackson attempted to use the words *kike* and *Hymie* in a song which the Jewish community found to be very offensive. The Jewish community demanded that the terms be removed and an apology to ensue. Consequently, Jackson removed the words and issued an apology. As wicked as the music industry may be, it does listen to and act on issues that could potentially affect their profitability. Even if the term was not removed for moral reasons, the Jewish community made a statement and maintained its respect, letting the world know that regardless of its context, casual use of those terms is unacceptable.

Other than the African American, no other race of people on the face of this earth stoops to the level of taking a demeaning and degrading word and affectionately use it when referring to one another. When one begins to understand the psychological impact behind this word and how it affects the psyche of Blacks and Whites alike, then and only then can an individual begin to comprehend the magnitude and bottomless depth of the adverse effects this term truly manifests upon the Black psyche.

The n-word is so strongly stigmatized that to try to redefine it would suggest that slavery and oppression never happened. The fact is it did. Black users of the n-word fail to realize that all other races have their own definition of the n-word, which is based on its historical meaning. To the world at large, "n**ger" symbolizes the Black race as an inferior freakish sub-human. As long as African Americans keep this word alive and keep alive the negative imagery as portrayed by rap artists of the Black race, the rest of humankind is going to be left little choice other than to believe and accept the perceived imageries.

African Americans' praising, worshiping and glorification of the n-word makes it more than just a word. It is as if the word is their Master, their God, to whom they willingly bow down. One black comedian, Paul Mooney, has boasted about how he brushes his teeth with the word and that it makes his teeth white. It is going to take much *mental* and *intestinal* fortitude for Black America to stand up and eliminate from its speech a 400-year-old mind control slave habit.

Though one may not personally use the word, but condones use of the term when other Black Americans use it in their presence and that person does not address the situation, that makes the receiver an accomplice to the on-going demise of the African American community. If a black person condemns non-blacks who use the n-word but look the opposite way when other Blacks use the term, that person is as much a mental-cripple as the user is.

An entire generation of young black people has grown up under the same negative influences as their enslaved predecessors. However, rather than being manipulated at the hands of crude and barbaric white slave masters, the mind control process has been resumed by black rappers and black hip-hop businessmen who have sold their souls and sold out Black America for the proverbial 30 pieces of silver.

Many gangsta rap songs use the n-word as a mantra every 10 seconds. This frequent use has been and is generally acceptable to the Black community. On the social media site Twitter, African Americans use the n-word—spelled with both the "a" and "er"—24 hours a day, 365 days a year.

Black n-word users, proponents or apathetics—whether high school drop outs or degreed professionals—feel an affinity toward the term and seem to be unable to free themselves from its clutches. The physically enslaved were left no choice but to identify with the n-word.

Today, African Americans have a choice, but rather than exercise the right to free self and society from this demonic term, far too many in the Black community continue to blindly embrace it and the helpless mentality. As the voice of proponents of the n-word grows louder, the fight against mental enslavement and the inability for a colossal percentage of Black America to acknowledge the effects of the n-word on their psyche is unnecessarily intensified.

It is also futile, naïve, irrational and downright asinine to assume that one can stop non-blacks from using the word while all at the same time promoting, marketing and commercializing the word globally. This act gives the entire universe the green light to use the n-word willy-nilly. And they do! How is it possible for so many Black Americans to be fools enough to go along with the antics of a few money hungry sell-outs who allow themselves to be used by controlling interests such as the music and movie industries? As a result of these sell-outs' multi-millionaire statuses, many in the Black community exalt them to high heaven signifying misplaced values and convictions as there is nothing honorable, respectable nor circumspect about selling out.

Many African Americans see these artists' and entertainers' success as a form of power and influence, failing to understand that these entertainers have attained this "success" at the *expense* of their community. Interestingly, as the Black community runs out and spends countless dollars to show their support and identify with one of their own, these entertainers rarely give back in a significant and impactful way to help turn the tide and face of the Black community.

Rather than promoting positive images; encouraging black youth not to take the same violent or negative routes that they took to stardom; stressing the importance of education, self-awareness, and self-dignity (having some class and sophistication); and truly being accessible to youths to serve as impressionistic mentors, they only continue to suck the life from the Black community in terms of asking citizens to buy their immoral records and empty labels with no positive messaging.

Another factor to point out is that if these people had the right type of power and influence that audiences really believe they do have, why when major issues occur in the Black community, do these influencers either refuse to forego being paid a few more blood dollars to stand up for what is right? Or, when they do decide to protest events in attempts of leveraging their supposed clout for something positive, it falls upon deaf ears and cannot cause a ripple in a baby's tub of bathwater?

Think about Jay-Z refusing to forego his business deal with Barney's in the wake of the racial profiling that occurred in early 2013, or the making of his CD album *N**gaz In Paris*. Money was and is more important to this guy than is the need to make a statement and really serve and support that community that has given so much to his success. As well, many black artists, rappers, and entertainers came forward to protest the murderous killing of Trayvon Martin, and even though their efforts were appreciated, their believed influence and power was, collectively, but a grain of salt in the fight.

Use and *tolerance* of the n-word is *not* indicative of a *free* mind nor the desire or effort to achieve greatness. Rather, embracing the n-word is reflective of a *bonded* mind or *mental* illness. However, this sickness is one that can be cured. The cure is found in the acquisition of knowledge that refutes any efforts to cast people of African descent in a negative light.

It starts with the realization that the city school systems, colleges, universities and the media are not going to provide the kind of information that will help build the self-esteem of a black student. Any external effort to help uplift the Black community would contradict the 400-year-old deracination indoctrination process. No traditional system in America is going to allow free-flow of an information stream that will free and release one's mind from American-European intellectual dominance.

African Americans have a responsibility and obligation to the sacred memories of their ancestors to be respectful and appreciative of their struggles, sacrifices, hardships, blood, sweat and tears. Their sacrifices, blood, sweat and tears have enabled contemporary Black African Americans—including rappers and entertainers, and all other Americans as well, to live the relatively good life experienced in these contemporary times. As such, rather than continuing to infuse mentalities of inferiority and status quo into future generations, which only leads to the continual demise of the collective Black community, Blacks must begin to teach and show by example future generations *a new way of thinking*. African Americans must also realize that with freedom, education and independence, comes the requirement to be *accountable* and *responsible* for one's own acts; in other words there is a crying need for the Black community to hold one another accountable which isn't *presently* done.

Contemporary Black America is still searching for its identity. This is proven in the hip-hop culture in their inability to recognize who they are; as such, they tend to relate to the lost gangsta-type, self-destructive images. Sadly, black youth have bought into this fabricated image. Black America's enlightened ones, from all walks of life, must address the lie and remove the deception to present an image of who and what they can truly be without selling their souls in the process.

Rather than blindly passing the proverbial and metaphorical n-word torch, the African American community should consider perceiving the n-word in different ways to determine for themselves the ideal use and implications or impact of the word:

- Use the n-word *only* when describing it in its historical context. Its history permanently disables its use as a "term of endearment." The drawback here is that very few people are qualified enough to lead a discussion about the word even among the ranks of educators.

- Seek knowledge and empowerment through continual self-education. Respect is rightfully earned by setting the proper example for others to follow, allow your actions and conduct to speak for you—*not* by just simply telling people they ought to respect you.

- Take note of how the n-word is marketed through music, songs, videos, and films, and how its use compares to other derogatory racial slurs. Then ask self these questions: Are other racial slurs used to such a great extent? Why is the n-word the only racial slur marketed globally? Could it be because Blacks are the only race who will *accept* the low standard of being degraded and ridiculed publicly?

Some people point to hip-hop's multicultural audience as not just providing comfort for past racial discrimination but in fact as a so-called cure. The melting pot of the hip-hop culture is suggested as a model for consummate racial justice, supposedly validating a so-called post-racial junction. Achievements such as those of an Oprah, a half dozen black CEO's of Fortune 500 companies, black mayors, the Congressional Black Caucus, Secretary of State, Supreme Court judge, NBA and NFL superstars, highly-paid black actors and actresses, and the election of Barack Obama tend to be viewed as examples of racism's total decline. However, in all cases, the mistake in this thinking is that the individual accomplishments are being viewed as collective advancement.

Although one does not argue the fact that seeing African Americans succeed is encouraging and motivating to other Blacks, much of the "I got mines" mentality still prevails in Black America. Until that selfish mentality is overcome with one of *collective* progression, the community will remain broken and a victim of racism. According to the NAACP's Criminal Justice Fact sheet http://www.naacp.org/pages/criminal-justice-fact-sheet:

African Americans now constitute nearly 1 million of the total 2.3 million incarcerated population, African Americans are incarcerated at nearly six times the rate of whites. Together, African American and Hispanics comprised 58% of all prisoners in 2008, even though African Americans and Hispanics make up approximately one quarter of the US population. According to Unlocking America, if African American and Hispanics were incarcerated at the same rates of whites, today's prison and jail populations would decline by approximately 50%. One in six black men had been incarcerated as of 2001. If current trends continue, one in three Black males born today can expect to spend time in prison during his lifetime, 1 in 100 African American women are in prison. Nationwide, African-Americans represent 26% of juvenile arrests, 44% of youth who are detained, 46% of the youth who are judicially waived to criminal court, and 58% of the youth admitted to state prisons (Center on Juvenile and Criminal Justice).

The country that holds itself out as the "land of freedom" incarcerates a higher percentage of its people than any other country. With statistics such as the aforementioned, how is it possible that the entire Black community has faced uninhibited progression with such "infrastructural breakdowns" occurring at extreme and persistent rates? The '60's Civil Rights Movement was about freedom from the oppressive discrimination that held Blacks back. Why hasn't that same steam of freedom been used to improve conditions for the group as a whole in present day? Moreover, is it possible that the influence of gangster rap and promotion of that lifestyle heavily contributed to the increased rates of imprisonment among Blacks?

True, the monetary achievements that some rap artists and black hip-hop businessmen have attained are remarkable; however, the means to which they used to make their mark is reprehensible, dishonorable, blasphemous and downright cowardly. Cowardly because they were not men enough to stand up against a systemic whose primary objective is to maintain a national objective that has *never been abandoned*. They have helped to further the perpetuation of mental exploitation and suppression of an unsuspecting group of people—Black African Americans.

Millions of young minds were, and still are, preyed upon and manipulated all for fame and fortune. They have been bombarded with negative, hopeless, and victimized images and messages of self; no promotion or encouragement of hope or power to take a stand and improve their lives is ever offered in these messages. Their sense of racial unity and cohesion has been corrupted, molding characters of self-hatred; only self-doubt, self-loathe, and distrust among their group has been engendered. Subsequently, Black unity has been pulverized and Black upward mobility for the collective group has been halted.

Ultimately, these men's shameless acts have single-handedly, but on a broad scale, contaminated the minds of the future generations of African Americans all in the name of making whatever sells on the market—regardless to its ramifications—to acquire their own riches. The point is that they have adversely-influenced the future torch-carriers in the Black community whether their actions were *intentional* or *not*. Artists have done nothing in using their influence to correct the problem or pull youths out of the pits of despair to re-direct youths in the proper way.

Collectively, as a *group*, the non-use of the n-word should be a no-brainer. African Americans should ALL be on the same page regarding use of the n-word. Whenever that word is openly used by any person of color, it serves as a reflection on the entire race of people. No matter whose mouth—black or non-black—the n-word idiom flows from, nothing cerebral, honorable, dignified, prideful or self-respectful exists from being submissive to and tolerant of its use. To allow one's self to be blinded by *monetary* success stories as a *substitute* for mental liberation and group attainment is the ultimate display of *stupidity* beyond belief.

Financially successful black rappers and businessmen are held in high esteem throughout the Black community. The products from which they have gained their wealth contribute to the corruption and pollution of the minds of many of black youth, crippling the minds of the impoverished even further. The building of *character* and the *positive molding* of young minds have taken a back seat to *cultural genocide* and *menticide*. The memories, sacrifices and struggles of African American ancestors too have been urinated, defecated and trampled upon at the expense of bestowing high applause upon those who have financially benefitted by selling out their race.

Though not all Black Americans use the pejorative n-word, far too many do. When one supports rappers and entertainers who humiliate and degrade their own race, in essence, that individual is participating in cultural and mental genocide. That supporter is contributing to the emotional, psychological, spiritual, and cultural extermination of the Black race. There perhaps is no argument or discussion more *senseless* than that of whether or not African Americans should use the n-word.

The fact that use of the n-word is even up for discussion is an *insult* to the sacred memories of Black ancestors who made it all possible through their blood, sweat, tears, struggles and sacrifices for all Americans to live in the greatest and strongest country on earth, the United States of America. It is past time for the descendants to start showing some *respect* and *gratitude* by tossing their self-centered, mean-spirited, ungrateful attitudes and use of the n-word in the trash can.

Some Black African Americans refuse to respect the sacrifices, struggles and honor of their ancestry. They will instead *defend* and *respect* those who desecrate and defile their ancestors' memories by embracing the n-word and making it a part of their everyday language and lifestyle. This is abominable and inexcusable.

Each individual Black American is honor-bound to turn their back on those entertainers and the industry that have made billions stomping on the dignity of Black African Americans, defiling the sacred memories of their ancestry, and poisoning the minds of Black youth. Most psychologists know that this kind of influence on young people breeds a desensitization to violence and deviant

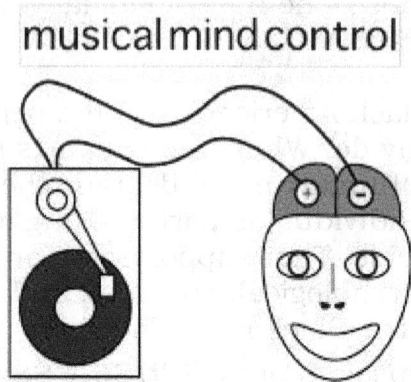

musical mind control

behavior. It is no coincidence that most of the music promoted includes violent lyrics that speak of Black-on-Black violence; the industry would likely not allow lyrics that promote Black-on-White violence or Black-on-gay attacks. In the initial stages of rap music, attempts were made at using lyrics pertaining to disrespecting police officers which was short lived. It behooves Black America to stop supporting an industry that continues to stifle intellectual development, and encouragement of active, collective progress as it relates to the Black community.

Ultimately, media giants and corporations are in business to make money. Any activity that supports that objective will be played up, promoted and sold like hot cakes to keep making their pockets fatter. On the other hand, any activity that negatively effects or even looks to threaten their wallet will be severed immediately. In February 2013, rap artist Lil Wayne came under fire for lyrics comparing the 1955 heinous, murderous beating of teenager Emmett Till to his sexual prowess when interacting with female genetalia; in May of the same year, he lost a multi-million dollar endorsement deal with PepsiCo's Mountain Dew as a result.

Emmett Till's family did not sit back, pass and allow Lil Wayne to have carte blanche to trample over and dishonor the death of their family member. By their speaking out and protesting the beverage company, events were placed into motion, which ultimately lead to the loss of Lil Wayne's endorsement deal.

Self-respecting people are tired of being sold out by heartless, money-hungry rappers. They are becoming less passive and apathetic about the images and messages being conveyed. They are now gaining the gumption to speak up and out against the undignified portrayals rappers promote. In April 2013, in the face of PepsiCo's situation, Reebok also decided to proactively sever ties with hip-hop artist Rick Ross because of his own offensive lyrics related to date raping women. Reebok smartly elected to forgo any negative publicity and resolved their potential issue before it could even become one.

Overall, these situations serve as testimony that when the Black community demands *responsibility* and *accountability* from their own as well as makes it known that they will not continue to allow media giants to promote that disrespect, people do listen. The subsequent results can be immediate, profoundly impactful, and have a huge domino effect.

For more than three centuries, it was beaten, tortured and forcibly instilled into Black African-Americans' minds to live, breathe, and heartily digest a self-hating,-destructing, -abasing and -abnegating personal image. This total embodiment and persona was then labeled n**ger/n**ga. With the aid of black sycophants, the indoctrination process continues non-stop to this very day; these sycophants serve as white-cloned ventriloquists who further facilitate the wanton acts of white supremacists from a deep, dark and ugly past. This continual effort of searching for ways to cast the n-word in a laudable light only further demonstrates the lack of *insensitivity, sense* and *appreciation* of the titanic battles that African American ancestry had to overcome.

The n-word carries the traumatic task and intent to destroy, maim or cripple a person of African descent. No matter how it is sliced, diced, or served up, once the smoke clears, the mission of this word is still intact. Use of the n-word is inappropriate and counterproductive to human relations and respect for everyone. Millions of educated, literate Blacks have not used the n-word under any circumstance on their way to prosperity and success in America. These are the true achievers in Black America who used their Black power to influence life success and create real opportunity for themselves, while also forging a deeply-engraved path founded on positivity, cultural pride, and dignity for generations to come. It's time to stop transferring a legacy of ignorance and apathy from one generation to the next.

Chapter 5

Wake up Everybody, Time to Teach a New Way

"Wake up everybody, no more sleeping in bed. No more backward thinking, time for thinking ahead...Wake up all the teachers, time to teach a new way. ...When you teach the children, teach them the very best you can. The world won't get no better—if we just let it be...we got to change it—Just You and Me."
~Harold Melvin and the Blue Notes

"It takes a village to make an impact, to make a difference, to change our world for the better."
~African Proverb

Consider a white hunter who sets out to capture a baby elephant. He stealthily approaches the baby and its mother with his eye and rifle aimed straight for the offspring. Sensing danger, the mother charges at the hunter who then raises his weapon against her, pulls the trigger, and kills the charging elephant. The baby elephant is captured and tranquilized. With a cable wrapped tightly around its neck, the elephant is taken into captivity where it is tied to a post. For five years, it remained tied to that post. Over this time frame, even though it had become full-grown, ten times the size of and stronger than its captors, the elephant did not realize it possessed the strength to uproot the post at any time and break free.

Instead, it had been *trained* to accept enslavement and felt that bondage was the norm. Finally, one day, it unintentionally broke free of the cable. Rather than scuffling off, the elephant chose to remain close to the post within its known confined parameters even though it was now free. The elephant elected captivity, *which is unnatural*, because it was so *accustomed* to being tied down and stuck in one spot.

This story is analogous to Black America's predicament in terms of its use of the n-word being the strong leash that keeps the community securely fastened to *mental enslavement*. Black Americans' use of the n-word is a result of being *conditioned, programmed* and *trained* to carry out the bidding of a manipulative racist society. Many Black African Americans really do not want or know how to be free because they are accustomed to their originally-allotted small fare.

Just as White America continued promoting and conducting slavery well after the Emancipation Proclamation—which was supposed to be a hard and immediate stop to all forms of slavery, the African American community has *allowed* an 18th century slave mentality to continue: Blacks have continued to promote and keep alive the demise of their community and stifled progression by use of the n-word; and yes through its low-vibratory energy the n-word has such power.

That term was created to hold Blacks in an inferior place in society and mental state of mind. As such, this line of thinking has caused learned helplessness, docility and passivity in the Black community, keeping many Blacks cerebrally anesthetized no matter the extent of education attained.

Many Blacks *have chosen* not to move away from the post, and, frankly, that is quite bewildering. How is it that so many in the Black community *have chosen* to remain captive and stationary when they are free to roam about unguarded? The *right* mix of KNOWLEDGE, UNDERSTANDING, and WISDOM enables one to move away from that figurative post and toward literal progress. Three essential components necessary for resurrection and empowerment to ultimate enlightenment are outlined below:

1) **Knowledge**: awareness of the facts, truth, and reality. Black America must undo the fables, lies and fantasies. Blacks as a people *are more committed* to fables, lies and fantasy than facts, truth and reality. This warped mentality stems from the outgrowth of a systemic indoctrination process and is a tremendous cause of many of the prevailing issues in Black America. Ironically, the Black male is more susceptible and vulnerable to this dilemma than his female counterpart.

2) **Understanding**: comprehending the "*right*" knowledge, and manifesting it into action. Once Black America gains the *correct* education, they must then learn to decipher and interpret these facts.

3) **Wisdom**: the optimum combination of knowledge and understanding expressed in the ability to decide right from wrong to make positive things happen. In other words, RATIONAL thinking must be applied and always prevail. Seeing yourself and your race as the n-word (n**ga) isn't an exhibition of RATIONAL thinking.

Acquiring this enlightenment should motivate one to become awakened and realize that they do have the power, strength, and capability to move away from that post or bondage. Certainly, no one within the systemic is going to tell Black America outright that they are truly free to go and create a life of fulfillment for themselves. Then again, no one is holding Black America in mental bondage, except Black America itself. Many remain captive because they have consciously *chosen not to* acknowledge and garner the elements needed for resurrection and empowerment. Instead, many choose to remain in their appointed position and as soon as they feel themselves venturing too far into an unknown, unfamiliar place, the programming kicks in and they willingly return to that familiar, confined place.

The modern day equivalent of remaining tied to the post lie in the *unwillingness* to divest one's self away from a 400 year old slave habit of paternalistic mannerisms and use of the n-word. People stay immersed in an 18th century slave mentality illusion because they really don't want to accept the *responsibilities* and *accountabilities* of freedom.

Black America has taken non-black man-made doctrines—rather, white man-made doctrines—as the inflicting rule and guide over and above facts and reality. Blacks have literally accepted that which does not even make sense as *fact* and *truth*. The methodology of chattel slavery has proven to be an experiment of brainwashing at its most pure, radical, systematic, and forceful best. Black African Americans' unhealthy willingness to self-sabotage serves as a testimony to the effectiveness of 300-plus years of mental abuse (mind control). To overcome this problem, a process that never took place must and needs to take place—legitimate psychotherapy.

A healing or re-emergence process should have been implemented to help Black Americans effectively cope with entering society under the guise of freedmen. The program should have addressed all aspects of slavery, provided psychological services to help Blacks overcome and cope with the torturous past and resources (ie, employment, shelter, education) to assist in establishing them as stable members of society. A number of Black psychologists such as The Osiris Group and Dr. Joy DeGruy can and do attest to the validity and need of a healing process that never occurred. [5]

Nonetheless, Black America cannot be hung upon on the *shoulda, coulda, woulda's*, nor can they remain victims of the much-needed psychotherapy process that did not happen. Rather, Black America must deal with the issue as it presently stands. The collective race must work to provide and find for themselves the education and resources needed to heal their confused mindsets and broken self-images caused by that 300-year plight. Each person must re-shape their mind so that they can effectively reform their realities and assist in returning Black America to a proud, self-respecting, unified and progressive group of people. By growing on a *rational* intellectual level, the standards of the community will be raised to newer and greater heights.

Black African Americans must decide that they are ready to love themselves. They must face their fear of *group* failure and commit themselves to the *collective* regardless to the eventual outcome. They must stop trying to prove themselves to others—which ends up causing them to sell out in the long run anyway. African Americans must instead start setting higher standards for themselves. After all, whites manage to live their lives without Black America's approval. Seeking self-respect, pride, dignity and honor is a good place to start.

The newly-enlightened will elect genuine thoughts of truth that allow real freedom of thought, raising the mind power, over the contaminating, false truth they have known for so long. The n-word is an evil word that served as a conduit to the physical and *mental* destruction of tens of millions of enslaved Africans during the African-American Holocaust, and continues to shackle the Black community today. Again, many may feel that the n-word carries no bearing on the Black community's existing situation, but this is exactly the belief the system wanted to instill in Black people.

The finest trick of the devil is to persuade you that he does not exist, Black America would be smart to take heed and realize that the effects of the n-word are real and that they have been duped into believing otherwise.

Everyone has a responsibility to act on behalf of their community's plight if they desire to experience change and true societal progression as each and every person is interconnected in some way.

The racial hierarchy was undergirded by an ideology which justified the use of *deceit, manipulation,* and *coercion* to keep Blacks "in their so-called place" of being a n**ger/n**ga. Every major societal institution has offered legitimacy to the hierarchy. Ministers preached that God had condemned Blacks to be servants. Scientists measured heads, brains, faces, and genitalia of Black men, seeking to prove that whites were genetically superior to Blacks. These types of experiments led to the 1994 publication of the well-received book, *The Bell Curve: Intelligence and Class Structure in American Life* throughout the American systemic.

White teachers—teaching only white students—taught that Blacks were less evolved cognitively, psychologically, and socially. The entertainment media, from vaudeville to television, portrayed Blacks as docile servants, happy-go-lucky idiots, and dangerous thugs; present day actors and actresses submissively help to keep the tradition alive.

These images have haunted Black America for a very, very long time. Unless the Black race exorcises the demons that these images have conjured up, they will never really be free as a group. Until Black African Americans are respected as a group, they as individuals are susceptible to discriminatory acts at any given time.

It is incredible how people support those who create works that encourage use of the n-word but chastise those who create works promoting non-usage of the pejorative term; opponents of the n-word are labeled as a so-called racist, conspirator, or are ridiculed. A strong, cogent mind will not succumb to the buffoonery of being manipulated and conforming to a lesser image of being someone's n**ga.

It is only African Americans that are encouraged and asked to accept base commonalities as a lifestyle. The question that must be answered pursuant to the same is *why?* Jews are not encouraged to embrace *kike* and *hymie;* Latinos are not encouraged to embrace *wetback* and *spic.* Only Black African Americans seem to naively and willingly agree to be referred to as a n**ga all due to a lacking sense of self-worth and no backbone.

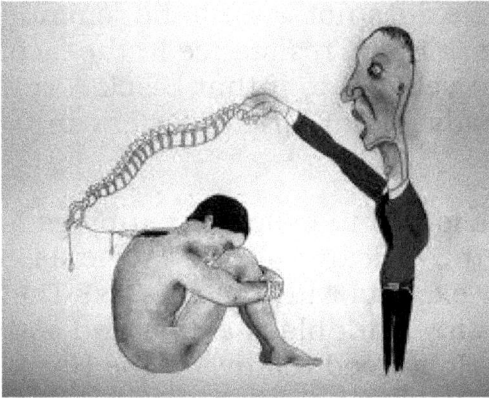

In addition, although the African-American Holocaust lasted three hundred-plus years longer and resulted in millions of more deaths than that of the Jewish Holocaust, many Black people, however, often hold greater regard and sympathy towards the Jewish Holocaust over their own. This display of low self-regard and even self-contempt among many Blacks is almost always accompanied with a higher regard toward whites. This displacement of empathy indoctrinated with misinformation, irrational and untrue beliefs is more evidence of a surviving 18th century slave mentality.

Hollywood serves as an instrument in helping to keep the 18th century slave mentality alive. Since 1915, cinema has always depicted Black America with a certain image beginning with the making of *The Birth of a Nation* on up into the 21st century making of such films as *Django, 12 Years A Slave*, and *The Butler*. The image that is alluded to is a *constant reminder* of the cruelty of Black subservience in America's slavery and Jim Crowism periods. Where is the redeeming value? There are a thousand stories of the Black experience lost to history that have a greater redeeming value than the experience of free black men stolen into slavery. The dominant culture does not want to be reminded of the power of *collective* Black resistance in the face of subjugation but yet sees to it that Black America is served up a steady diet of African-American *subservience*.

No other race is forced to have their subjugation recounted like the African American; where is the sharing of their exploits with the masses? There was a time when the only work black actors and actresses qualified for in Hollywood relative to the Black experience was playing a slave, servant, some form of a Stepin Fetchit character, or a carefree knee-slapping dumb bunny. In this 21st century movies regarding the *Black experience*, nothing has changed.

Hollywood's failure to promote stories about enslaved Africans *resistance* against subjugation is belittling and denigrating. Where is the balance in telling these stories of cultural significance? When it comes to use of the n-word and imagery of slavery, there is always the rallying cry that history cannot and should not be sanitized from Blacks and Whites alike. Agreed history should not be sanitized, so why is the *fighting spirit, resistance* side of slavery never, ever projected on the silver screen?

On a more prideful and serious level, there also exists hundreds of stories of African Americans overcoming adversity through becoming great innately-talented inventors, entrepreneurs, entertainers, and statesmen. There are positive aspects about the musical experience of the Blues, Jazz, etc. emanating out of Memphis, Tennessee; and the Deep South in general. Why is there not a steady diet of these stories shared in cinema to balance out the reinforcement of Black/African American *subservience*? The reason Hollywood gets away with this is because Black America in general is still sound asleep.

Moreover, white people have faced oppression at points in history, but these stories are also never shared. Is the infrastructure fearful that if they publicize Black power/triumph and white subservience, the tables will turn? Are they concerned that Black/African Americans will realize their truest worth and white people will be humbled in knowing that they too were mistreated and considered the downcast inferior people? During the 8th and 9th centuries of the Fatimid Caliphate, most of the slaves were Europeans (called Saqaliba) captured along European coasts and during wars. [16]

Could they be concerned that in the wake of sharing these stories—revealing the unabridged, unveiled truth—that a real cultural respect will be realized and true equality will be attained? At whose expense or benefit are these stories not being shared? Wake up, America! The systemic continually works day and night to keep not just Black America *in their place* but also anyone else who would be on board with total mental liberation and freedom.

As usual, Black America is being strong-armed, bamboozled, and hoodwinked. American history has always been sanitized wherever it suits the purpose of White America. Hollywood serves as an institution to maintain and uphold the hoodwinking of Black America. Not only does Hollywood sanitize history in the making of movies, they will and do completely ignore certain aspects of history in general. Why aren't movies ever made that illustrate legendary heroes such as John Horse and the Black Seminole Indians, and/or Haiti's General Toussaint L'Ouverture, who defeated both Napoleon and the British superpower armies?

In spite of all the adversities and calamities enslaved Africans were forced to endure, they demonstrated an unrelenting capacity to survive, overcome and prevail despite the overwhelming odds. From the ashes of despair arose a solid, magnificent race of people embodying the very essence of genuineness, pride, dignity, and perseverance, the African American. Negro spirituals, blues and jazz were created to help Black African Americans maintain a sense of internal calmness and hope during strife; cultivate, embrace and express individuality; and serve as living connections to and trophies of cultural history, knowledge and heritage.

With this vigor of relentless resilience and faith at their core, the enslaved captives continued to defy barriers and become fruitful and respected contributors in society by taking on such roles as inventors, entrepreneurs, scholars, writers, religious and political leaders, athletes, entertainers, teachers, doctors, lawyers and scientists. Why aren't black producers and directors capturing these moments on film? Why are they sitting back allowing white Hollywood to control and manipulate the imagery of Black/African Americans?

If Black America thinks for one second that if a white director or producer were to make such movies that it would not be sanitized, they are terribly disillusioned. So, then where are the *black* directors and producers who will stand up to present the real, unadulterated truth? Instead of Tyler Perry giving America a heavy dose of the cackling *Madea* and other black directors coming up with those one dimensional slave movies, they should be leveling the playing field by presenting all aspects of the Black/African American experiences. The hope is also that the excuse of securing proper funding to back such projects is not the problem. If funds can be secured to make the one-sided movies or other cinema that do not even look at such serious issues, can funds not be secured to convey the other side of the coin on the large screen? Moreover, it is projected that by 2015, Black America will be spending more than a trillion dollars annually. Clearly the funds are and will continue to be available—but perhaps not the desire.

More movies need to be made such as the likes of Haile Gerima's *Sankofa,* which by the way was not produced in Hollywood. Spike Lee is also given credit for at least coming out with *Malcolm X.* This was proven to be one of Denzel Washington's best performances, although an argument could be made for his performance in *Hurricane* as well. Yet in spite of these two very powerful performances, he wins an Oscar for a more diminished performance portraying a rogue cop in *Training Day.* Hollywood is all about image. Clearly, the image of Black America is being carefully manipulated and orchestrated. Wake up Black America! While you are just "playing to play," the ruling class is "*playing to win,*" and that's to keep the African American community in a subjugated and paternalistic state of mind.

Given the historical record of negative African American imagery and the current nebulous climate of Hollywood, as well as the music industry, any black person with any form of power should be very selective in ideas they support and materials they produce. Too many black youth are being bombarded with negative images; as such, it's imperative for the Black/African American community to start taking control of the group's own fate and destiny. Stand up! Stand tall! Walk erect! Be proud! Stop being weak, feeble-minded going along just to get along. Getting along is fine unless there is a price.

In other words, stop accepting the concept that to be Black means to be somebody's n**ger/n**ga. This is 2014, not 1814; lose that 18th century slave mentality. Stop giving power and being subservient to those whose only objective is to maintain a 400-year-old policy of keeping Blacks in a so-called place of submissive inferiority, discard the *Django* Stephen's image.

Black African Americans have been subjected to a massive psychological and physical trauma that has continued uninterrupted from the 17th century on into this 21st century. Below are some examples from the misfortunes of being categorized as a n**ger. These examples are not anomalies. Quite the contrary, for more than 300 years such incidents were common-place and always with the delirious chanting of the n-word ringing in the victims' ears as they gasped for their last breaths:

- In 1904, black sharecroppers Luther Holbert and his wife were chained to a tree. An audience of 600 white spectators enjoyed fine treats such as deviled eggs, lemonade and whiskey in a festive atmosphere while Mr. and Mrs. Holbert underwent atrocious and purely evil acts: first their fingers were chopped off one by one, then their ears, followed by a severe beating that left Mr. Holbert with one eye dangling from its fractured socket. Next, "spirals...of raw, quivering flesh" were extracted from both Holberts with a corkscrew before the couple was finally burned alive. As they drew on their last breaths, the last words they heard was the ranting of "n**ger, n**ger, n**ger."

- To condition and program the minds of small children, one method used was to gather groups of kids around a pregnant black woman. With her hands tied and hanging from a meat hook, her stomach would be cut open and the embryo pulled out and killed. Witnessing such a grotesque event of course would traumatize a young kid's mind. Forcing them to behold such an atrocious act was the intent and purpose of planting fear and an inferiority complex into their hearts, minds and souls.

- In 1955, a 14-year-old kid from Chicago by the name of Emmett Till was visiting relatives in Mississippi. He made the fatal mistake of whistling at a white woman. In the middle of the night, he was kidnapped from the home he was visiting, taken to the woods and bludgeon to death. One of his eyes was gouged out before he was shot through the head and his body disposed of in the Tallahatchie River; his murderers weighted the mutilated body with a 70-pound (32 kg) cotton gin fan tied around his neck with barbed wire. His body was discovered and retrieved from the river three days later.

Malcolm X once said that "the worst thing racism did was to make us hate ourselves." The continued usage of the word n**ger/n**ga provides no greater example of this self-hatred! White supremacy is not a bunch of ignorant rednecks who hate Blacks. It is a *system*, a *religion* that is used to eliminate the threat of white genetic annihilation.

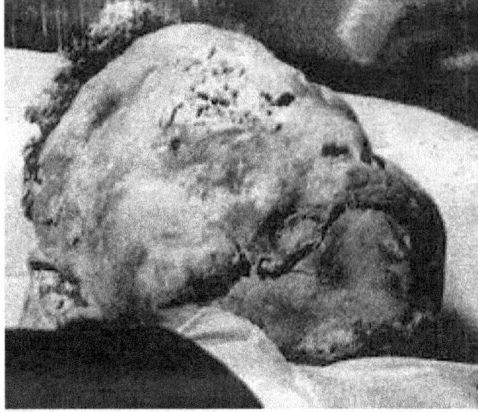

Picture of 14 year old Emmett Till who in 1954 was brutally murdered for whistling at a white woman while visiting in Mississippi.

The moment has arrived to awaken the intellect and potential that lives within African Americans' current and future generations. The only way to achieve this feat is by ensuring the freedom and uplifting of a diminished mindset; and the only way to achieve true freedom is by relinquishing the hold to any remnants of the enslaved past—and that *includes* the n-word.

The future of the African-American community lies in the hands of the black youth. Black adults must learn to understand the importance of infusing young spongy minds with positive thoughts and images, for they are the wave of the future. Every day, all across the country, Black African American students from grade school on up to and into college are being conditioned to refer to themselves as n**gahs. This is not positive reinforcement—it is an uninterrupted path to prolonged menticide.

It's hard to die. It's painful to die. However, the n-word must die in order for the Black race to truly live. The n-word does not want to die, but the chains of bondage must be broken and any remnant of that bondage—including the n-word—must be buried and allowed to rest in peace. Then, like a mighty phoenix, Black

America can arise from the ashes of mental subjugation and soar to the heights once known and experienced by Black forefathers of the ancient golden age.

A man is not truly free until the shackles of the human mind, body and spirit are broken. Freedom is manifested in the ability to free self from any hindrance such as the n-word. Until one is capable of taking control of their own mind and thoughts, they are *still* a slave. During the days of physical enslavement, many Blacks refused to be mentally enslaved despite their physical circumstance. Fortunately, this is still the case today to a great degree; *not all* Black African Americans suffer from an 18th century slave mentality. Sadly, though, the majority have not the mental nor intestinal fortitude to overcome the effects of mind control as is validated by their attitude towards the use of the n-word. And will go to any length to defend their use of the pejorative term.

The number *one* priority for the African American community should be an unconditional commitment to the *psychological* and *spiritual* liberation of all Black African Americans. It begins with the burial of the n-word. No, the word cannot be made to vanish into thin air, but it can be made to vanish from the speech of all Black Americans.

Frederick Douglas: Torch holder of *the* new way

In Frederick Douglass' July 5, 1852, Fourth of July speech, he resolved to the audience:

> *"What, to the American slave, is your 4th of July? I answer; a day that reveals to him, more than all other days in the year, the gross injustice and cruelty to which he is the constant victim. To him, your celebration is a sham; your boasted liberty, an unholy license; your national greatness, swelling vanity; your sound of rejoicing are empty and heartless; your denunciation of tyrants brass fronted impudence; your shout of liberty and equality, hollow mockery; your prayers and hymns, your sermons and thanks-givings, with all your religious parade and solemnity, are to him, mere bombast, fraud, deception, impiety, and hypocrisy — a thin veil to cover up crimes which would disgrace a nation of savages. There is not a nation on the earth guilty of practices more shocking and bloody than are the people of the United States, at this very hour.*
>
> *Go where you may, search where you will, roam through all the monarchies and despotisms of the Old World, travel through South America, search out every abuse and when you have found the last, lay your facts by the side of the every-day practices of this nation, and you will say with me that, for revolting barbarity and shameless hypocrisy, America reigns without a rival."*

Frederick Douglass' speech personifies the indomitable spirit of the 18th and 19th century slaves. They refused to accept any beliefs and participate or rejoice in superficial, conciliatory occurrences that seemed to mock or minimize the sacrifice and struggle countless ones endured in the very same nation that was built by their tireless toil but refused to allow them to enjoy the fruit of their labor.

This same unrelenting spirit of truth, remembrance, and striving toward one's own superior entitlement was prevalent in freed descendants throughout the 1960's. Though physically barred during the 18th and 19th century, African Americans were less mentally enslaved then than many Blacks of this 21st century. A vast amount of 21st century Blacks have in many ways performed a180-degree turnaround from the unrelenting and striving spirit of the '60's; one of the more prevalent regressing moves is in their desire to embrace a dehumanizing, demented, degrading term laced with carnage and immorality: *the* n-word.

One cannot visualize from any depth or corner of one's essence or mind Frederick Douglass, father of America's Civil Rights Movement, or any other victimized enslaved ancestor finding embracement of the n-word acceptable by their descendants. Such an embracement serves as an indictment that even though the slaves were supposedly freed in 1865, 145 years later many African Americans are still mentally enslaved. That is a *depressing* and *disgusting* thought. The indoctrination of the black slaves' forcible use of the n-word has proved to be a self-refueling and self-generating mind control mechanism.

Black leaders of the sanctioned slave era and leaders of the 1960's demonstrated much courage and intestinal fortitude in their efforts to unshackle the minds of their enslaved black brothers and sisters. Today, the presence of true Black African American leaders with the same conviction and determination to overcome seems to be non-existent. The system has found a way to keep any would-be leaders silent. The system architects have devised strategies that ensure some

Blacks' obedience to the current status as they help to suppress and exploit their own kind, keeping them in an uncouth state of mind.

White America no longer has to physically wield the whip to keep a race of people enslaved; rather, White America continues to maintain the system by supporting Black America's degradation through compensating entertainers, scholars, athletes and the like to continue perpetuation of the brainwashing process in a variety of ways. In turn, these black ventriloquists continually work to mute the voices of the enlightened few by believing and loudly conveying to their followers that *no power exists* in the n-word or other forms of cultural genocide.

Yes, Blacks are the ones exhorting other African Americans to remain in and accept a pre-arranged place of being the n-word. Sadly, many Blacks do not realize that until *all* Blacks are liberated from mental enslavement, no African American will ever be able to experience the fullness and goodness of *true* equality. Henry Louis Gates, Jr., Ph.D., the Harvard professor arrested and accused of breaking into his own home, discovered this truth first-hand. Dismally to report, his case is no anomaly, and so long as he and other African Americans see themselves as the n-word that is how they are going to be treated.

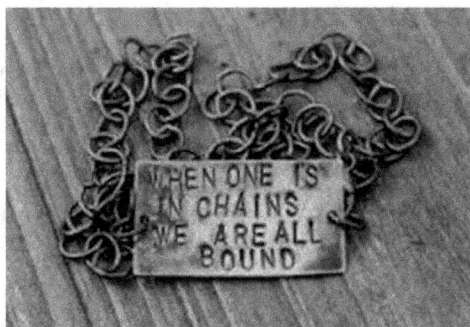

White America had, for centuries, instilled into the minds of the slaves and a freed Black America that the term "black" was something in which to be ashamed, something evil and of no value. In the '60's, Black America took the notion to become free of such terms as *Negro* and *Colored*, and adopted the terms *Black* and *African American*. Black people of the '60's realized the mind game being played on them, and had the strength and fortitude to overcome this falsified negative mentality. They realized the beauty and strength of their blackness, and used it as a shield, weapon, and faith to march toward and re-claim their God-given liberties.

Current Black America has retrogressed and no longer exhibits the heart and soul of the '60's; instead, they prefer to surrender, meekly lie down, and submit to a term that keeps them *mentally enslaved*. As recently as November 2013, NBA greats Charles Barkley, Shaquelle O'Neal and ESPN commentator Michael Wilbon, bowed down to the n-word—a word that dehumanized, stigmatized and objectified their ancestors—and pledged their allegiance to it on national TV.

During the '60's, the gallantly-fought battle was against social injustice and Jim Crowism. Even though today's struggle continues to hinge heavily on a more subtle form of social injustice, Black America has the potential to unite and overcome these issues collectively. However, this unity can only be achieved once the group collectively awakens from the 400 years of mind manipulation and willfully cuts away all attachments and long-standing addictions to the past, including use of the n-word. Just as 300 plus years of slavery and Jim Crowism was no joke, African Americans' use of the pejorative n-word is no laughing matter.

A little more food for thought: The senseless beatings of the enslaved were a way to break the Black man's spirit just as referring to him as a n**ger/n**ga was to accomplish. To say that the use of the n-word no longer has power because Blacks have so-called reclaimed it is like saying being physically enslaved and beaten aimlessly has no power because Blacks are now the ones conducting the enslaving and beating. Really, Black America? *Please, wake up!*

Those are insane justifications and excuses no matter what angle, perspective, or light in which one considers either thought. A whipping is a whipping no matter who delivers or receives it, and it hurts every time it happens! One may learn to numb her/himself to the blows, but guaranteed, every blow lands with some intensity of impact and leaves bruises, cuts, and scars— physical impoverishment, broken communities and inferior mentalities.

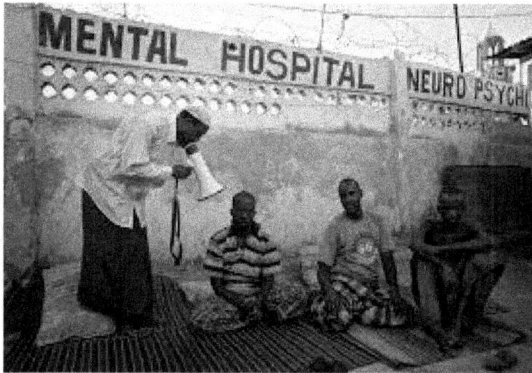

A man isn't truly free until the shackles of the human mind, body and spirit are broken. Until one is capable of taking control of their own mind and thoughts, he is still a slave. Black America is not in control of its own destiny as is evidenced by its use of the n-word.

Frederick Douglass once said: *"Where justice is denied, where poverty is enforced, where ignorance prevails, and where any one class is made to feel that society is...to oppress, rob and degrade them, neither persons nor property will be safe."*

The psychological and spiritual liberation of all Black people and realization of true independence will only be obtained through embracing a reality of truth and enlightenment. This liberation will not happen through the embracement of the n-word. Is today that day of mental independence?

The future for winning this anti-n-word battle, but most importantly the war against *mental enslavement* and communal degradation, looks promising. Every day there are signs sprinkled throughout Black America that Black folks are gaining the confidence to break the chains of *mental enslavement.* Entertainers who once used the term have made public commitments to denounce use of the idiom; some hip-hop artists have begun to develop and market songs with the crux of them stressing that Black is beautiful; and youths and organizations are even taking pledges not to use the n-word in their daily interactions.

Each and every day, more and more Black African Americans are *waking up, standing up* and *cleaning up* their act to declare their autonomy and independence by detaching themselves from that incorrigible word n**ga/n**ger. Some are beginning to accept the reality that no shame exists in acknowledging how they may have viscerally embraced the pejorative term in the past. They are now indeed clear that the shame lies in the refusal to divest one's self from its unforgiving clutches. Knowing that mistrust was beaten into Black Americans should cause each person of color to begin to question why unfounded distrust pervades one's psyche; by raising the question, the answers will begin to come and in clear form. Subsequently, the wounds will begin to heal.

Reform in the Black community is on the rise, but it will take the collective community's energy for the efforts to gain real traction and have lasting positive effects.

Chapter 6

The N-word is a Contrivance for Mind Control

"It is of vital importance to be careful of what goes into the subconscious mind. Words and thoughts that are repeated often get stronger by the repetitions, sink into the subconscious mind and affect the behavior, actions and reactions of the person involved."

~Remez Sasson

Whenever the "massa" gave the subjugated something, no matter what it was, he took it—whether voluntarily or by coercion. Sadly, no matter how demeaning or dreadful the thing may have been, he had no choice but to accept the token, allowing it to become a part of his identity. For instance, the Black man was categorized as a 'n**ger' by the massa. When asked, "What is your name?" the slave responded: "N**ger." "What? Say it loud so they all can hear you, what is your name?" the master would demand; and in an even louder and convicted voice the slave would affirm, "N**ger!!!" And yet again when he was asked, he replied solemnly: "I am a N**GER."   Finally, the white man said, "Right!! That's a good n**ger. *Never ever forget*—who and what you are—and your appointed place."

Today, as opposed to being ruthlessly, physically and emotionally beaten into submission and acceptance of the n-word by a brutal white social system, black people find themselves courted and conned by other Blacks to voluntarily remain in their pre-appointed place of a n**ger/n**ga. In this contemporary era, white supremacy is most effective when it uses a black voice as a ventriloquist, and today, many rappers, comedians and black scholars eagerly fulfill the part.

It is incredulous and appalling how some black scholars encourage their college students to greet each other as n**gahs. An uninterrupted indoctrination process that began almost 400 years ago by a brutal racist social system is now carried on by cloned black representatives. The definition of self is only limited by who that person believes themselves to be, and far too many African American scholars—who are, by definition of their roles, leaders and influencers in the community—have a diminished image of themselves and their race.

The American institutionalized systemic has always identified Black America with the n-word and, therefore, find Black Americans' willingness to accept and relate to their pre-appointed place and category of being a n**ger/n**ga gratifying, ease on their guilty conscience, and proof that Black America accepts its so-called appointed place.

So long as black people restrict themselves to saggin' pants, referring to one another as n**ger/n**ga, b*tches, MF's, and limiting their admirations and symbols of success to sex, cars, drugs, guns, sports and life in the 'hood, all is well in the American institutionalized systemic. However, a far more challenging and graver concern to the systemic are Black Americans retaking control of their minds, demonstrating the ability to think and act *rationally*, and possessing demeanors of royalty—walking with dignity. Those who boldly declare their independence and rightfully return any unfitting or cursed gifts to the systemic—one primarily being the n-word—are the one's considered a virus to the system.

Black historians and scholars such as Dr. Asa Hilliard, Dr. John Henri Clarke, Dr. Chancellor Williams, Dr. Richard Williams, Dr. Amos Wilson, Dr. Kwaku Person-Lynn, Dr. Ray Higgins, Dr. David Pilgrim and a few others serve as examples of liberated, independent thinkers. As such, the American institutionalized systemic refrains from parading these gentlemen's names before a sound-asleep Black community in fear that the knowledge of these thinkers may awaken the slumbering masses.

However, they will parade and promote the likes of a Dr. David Bradley, Dr. Randall Kennedy, certain rappers, black comedians and some other hand-picked high profile Blacks—all of whom are proponents of the n-word—before an unsuspecting and sleeping African American community. The systemic will and does make every effort to keep the sycophants—n-word supporting Blacks—constantly before the public to mislead others into remaining blinded to the truth even though they erroneously think they are in control of their thoughts and aware of the situation that is occurring.

Seldom, if ever, are anti-n-word activists paraded before a snoozing Black community. It should be pointed out that during the '60's, African American leaders had carte blanche access to their community via the news media; the systemic has since then instituted controls that allow only messages by cloned white messengers with black skin to reach the masses of African Americans. In other words, if it was in the best interest of the systemic for black folks *not to* embrace the n-word, the full weight of the news media would swing into action *supporting* an anti-n-word campaign. Within less than 90 days or so of that type of campaign, black users of the n-word would be persuaded to stop embracing the *demeaning, degrading,* and *dishonorable* n-word. Instead, media coverage is always given to Blacks who are proponents and promoters for use of the n-word.

The mis-use of Christianity also plays a role in the over-all scheme of the current conflict. The belief was that by viewing Blacks as sub-humans (n**gers), Whites would be justified in the eyesight of their God to perform any inhumane acts on them they so deemed appropriate to commit. Butchering, slaughtering, mutilating, brutally raping, boiling and burning people alive; disemboweling with hot pokers; and, of course, hangings were just a few of the so-called "justifiable" acts carried out against the enslaved. Up to as recently as the '60's, use of the n-word by southern whites was not intended as a racial slur. It served as a code word among them that they were interacting with some inhumane species, and, therefore, whatever action inflicted upon black people, in their morbid minds, was justifiable.

Slaves, in reverent fear of God submit yourselves to your masters, not only to those who are good and considerate, but also to those who are harsh.
-I Peter 2:18

When white slave masters taught religion to slaves, the parts of the Bible they referenced most were the ones that told people to be patient, wait for Heaven, obey their slave-masters while on earth and that someday the meek will inherit the earth.

The steady conquest and enslavement of a whole people made it imperative to create both a *religious* and a "*scientific*" doctrine to assuage the white conscience. During the 1960's Civil Rights Movement, feeling their grip of mind control slipping away, white clergymen chastised Martin Luther King for his leadership role in the movement. Since the days of chattel slavery, the black clergy was always used as a source to help keep the African American population mentally crippled.

When Rev. King deviated from the norm, the white clergymen saw it as a form of an abomination and sacrilegious for him to not only be involved in the Civil Rights Movement but even more so its leader. Indeed all of America had been taken by surprise and caught off guard, the 400 year old anesthesia effect on African Americans was beginning to wear off and like a sleeping giant was slowly waking up. So what happened? White America recovered, administered some more anesthesia and the drowsy giant (African Americans) slipped back into another coma and haven't awaken since.

Each time African Americans refer to one another as a "n**ger" or "n**ga" in a sense of so-called endearment, they desecrate and dishonor the memories and spirits of their enslaved forefathers, forgetting their history and the great pains and struggles they suffered in and for this country. It is current day black people's duty and call to accord their ancestors a better place in the Black race's collective memory.

Black America must continue to follow-up and relentlessly work toward changing the thinking of their community—the young and the old, and drive them to more positive and noble pursuits. The Black community must share the serum of healthy self-respect with others most in need of hope. African Americans can have tremendous impact and become that agent of change.

However, they collectively must first believe they have the ability to make the change, and take strides at every level to re-program the group's psyche to restore the dignity, respect, and cultural pride that once reigned at the very essence of the Black race. This will only come about through self-policing, holding one another accountable and responsible as is expected of non-blacks.

Becoming indignant and upset at non-blacks' use of the n-word after allowing Black America and mainstream media to promote, market and commercialize the word globally is being irresponsible and unaccountable for the behaviors one's own actions perpetuated—it is irrational and insensible. Black African-American users of the word opened the door and everybody is walking through it. Their use of the term has all other races jumping at the chance to openly and defiantly use a word that demeans and degrades each individual African-American person, and everything the group represents including culture and heritage. Succinctly, African American users of the n-word have succeeded in making all African Americans the laughing stock of the world.

Younger generations have grown up in a society that has used the word as common language their whole lives. They seem to have become desensitized to the term and ignorantly use it not knowing they are foolishly carrying on a 400-year-old extirpation plight. Just because they have heard its use their whole lives does not make use of the term right nor does it downplay or eradicate its effects. Similarly, just because one grows up in the house with an alcoholic parent, then as an adult they drink alcohol their whole life— picking up the habit from their parent—does not make the activity right nor does it soften its effects—one will still end up with cirrhosis of the liver and die.

What advantage is there in referring to self as a n**ga? If this somehow makes an African American feel connected to other black people, all should consider themselves slaves on the plantation with no hope of escape.

If no other efforts are made in the very near future, decide to at least *stop* using the n-word to characterize self; describing other black people one may feel is somehow inferior to them; or in reference to a loved one—masquerading the term as a form of endearment, which is an empty sign of self-hatred.

Granted old habits can be very difficult to break, much less a 400-year-old slave habit. Some Black African Americans are so addicted to the n-word that they cannot allow 24 hours to pass without using it at some point. Consequently, eliminating use of the term is going to be far more difficult for some than others, which is why black people are going to have to help one another overcome this human tragedy. No need to chide users of the word; lead by example and kindly let them know that the same is expected of them. As long as the weaker, feeble-minded users are not being encouraged to use the disparaging term, they will soon take heed to the message and stop.

The n-word is associated with a brutal social system that denied Black African Americans humanity; they were marked as things, not human beings. Do not forget slavery did not end with the Emancipation Proclamation. The harsh reality is that the brutal world of slavery continued for almost another century, finally coming to an end in the early 1960's. During the '60's civil rights struggles, many southern whites viewed Blacks wandering from their so-called place of being n**gers as them having the nerve to think they were real humans as opposed to being sub-human. As a consequence, young black men in the South were often stopped and harassed by law enforcement officers. These so-called lawmen would ask these innocent men their names and if they did not reply with "I AM A N**GER," they were beaten until those words flowed from their swollen and bloody lips.

Many Blacks today think this is all funny and take themselves and the n-word *as a joke*. This lack of a healthy self-esteem stems from the minstrel days where Blacks were coerced into not taking themselves seriously. That simulated demeanor lingers to this very day for many Black African Americans.

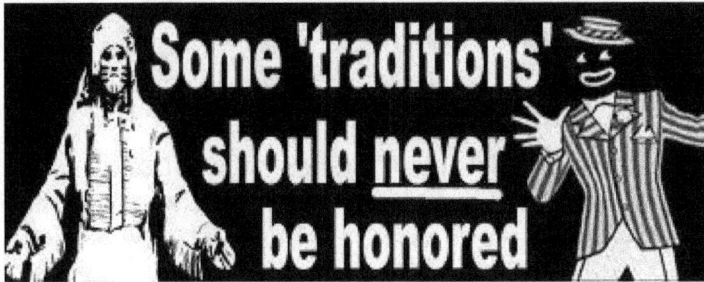

Some 'traditions' should <u>never</u> be honored

Hurling the epithet n**ger at civil rights demonstrators was not done solely to insult. It was a twisted way for biased whites to justify to themselves the pointless beatings, releasing of police dogs, use of high-pressure fire hoses on the black protesters, and fondling of black women who had been jailed for their participation in the civil rights demonstrations. To the racist protesters, Blacks were sub-humans, inhuman; and as such, their unconscionable, inhumane acts were deemed acceptable to them.

During the 1960's, Black America was vibrant, sagacious, intolerant, circumspect and self-respectful. The positive attributes were endless. The *intestinal and mental fortitude* of '60's Black America was unwavering. Unfortunately, 21st century Black America seems to *lack* the same conviction or determination to continue to strive for and demand ultimate respect and equality. Instead, they kowtow to demean and degrade themselves with no sense of self-respect.

Why the disparity in attitude and mental fortitude between African Americans of the '60's and 21st century Black African Americans? By accepting Dr. King's message of integration while forgetting Malcolm X's message of economic independence, Black America effectively committed itself to a more sophisticated form of *mental enslavement*. White America's elites' practice of economically exploiting and suppressing its Black population were never actually abandoned. It was reincarnated into a more sophisticated contemporary and stealthy design that provides a more socially-acceptable means to covertly control and suppress the advancement of the African-American population.

Unless the masses of African Americans are made more aware of America's true ruling elites and their modern methods and practices of economically exploiting and suppressing the Black population, nothing will change even with being led by a black President. Black African Americans' sole salvation—as a group—is economic independence without which equality is *guaranteed* to always be an elusive entity.

However, economic independence cannot be achieved without first building a foundation of *pride, dignity, honor* and *self-respect.* There are no shortcuts to establishing this foundation that must only be founded on all things positive. Any remnants or references associated with anything negative must be excluded as a material in structuring this pivotal, long-standing life source. As such, the use of the *dis-respectful* n-word is one of those materials that must be excluded in order to erect a sturdy, cohesive base.

For the past 30 plus years, an element of ruin has taken over Black America while the silent majority sits back, watches and allows the community's annihilation to endure uninterrupted. The time has come for the silent majority to wake up, stand up, and help clean up a mess created by proponents of a self-destructive mind set. The key and lasting culprit at the very core of that chaos is the n**ga mentality.

Today, many African Americans find it *acceptable* to be referred to as the n-word as if it is some sort of *badge of honor* to be proudly worn. Then there are the non-users who will condone others' use of the term by sitting idly and saying nothing. They sit quietly and watch as drugs, misogyny, saggin' pants, crime and violence are marketed and promoted as a way of life. They act as if this type of lifestyle is all synonymous with being Black. Rappers Jay Z and Kanye West's *N**gas in Paris* music release serves as an example of absolute impassivity on the part of the Black community. Where was the Black community's outrage in this situation? The lack of outrage was far more disconcerting than the song title itself.

Much confusion exists about how to define the n-word.

Some assume that Webster's Dictionary *accurately* defines the pejorative term; unfortunately, such an assumption is a misguided one. Over the years, Webster's whimsical definition of the n-word has changed countless numbers of times. What has never changed is the immutable diabolical history of the word; its past serves as a true and clear definition of the anathematized term available to anyone willing to invest the time and effort to research a history that has been sanitized by the academic powers in place.

The truth of the matter is that when it comes to slavery and the n-word, history has *always* been sanitized and distorted in efforts to lighten the deliberate blows of hate, hostility and genocide that were carried out against Blacks. It is as if the historians are saying slavery was bad, but not that bad. Honestly, it is somewhat an irreverence to be sanctimonious about the removal of the n-word from *Huckleberry Finn* and fail to exhibit the same concerns about the marginalization of Black American and World history in general.

The effort should be to show current generations the ignorance that was acted out in the past, the sickness the use of the n-word bores in all, and how to effectively proceed today by eradicating the n-word from their use. The truth in history is supposed to make people stronger and serve as a fundamental building block for improvement; however, when one models self after lifestyles such as that promoted in the hip-hop culture, the opposite is pathetically manifested.

To masquerade the n-word as a term of endearment is a sign of an on-going disability to break away from an instilled and eventually cultivated self-hatred. Use of the idiom serves as a psychological conduit to negatively manipulate and shape the minds and collective perceptions of America's black population to perceiving an unfavorable and false perception of self. Descendants of slavery suffer from such severe psychological scars of slavery. These very visible marks of systemic inferiority have been blindly passed down through generations via slave mentalities. The same slave mentalities have caused many Black Americans to become immune to the idea of debasing themselves; they think nothing wrong of defining themselves with a word that is drenched in carnage and bloodshed.

Myrlie Evers-Williams, wife of slain prominent Mississippian Civil Rights leader Medgar Evers, has spoken out against use of the n-word by all Americans. Particularly, though, Mrs. Evers-Williams shows gravest concern regarding Black Americans' use the word, which is understandably the most disturbing and damaging in her perspective. As Mrs. Evers-Williams concludes in an article she wrote: "The word should never leave your mouth... That bothers me more than a Caucasian using it. It is racist. It is hateful. It is everything it was meant to be."

Why all the fuss *over a word?* Many will and do ask. Some Black Americans believe there are more important issues in the Black community that one should turn one's attention to rather than the use of a word. However, this term is one of the most prominent issues because its existence and use continues to contribute to the inferior mindsets that plague the Black community. Use of the n-word ultimately perpetuates the cycle of demise; as well, it chastises all the sacrifice and death brought about in the Black community in fighting for equality, justice, and true freedom.
What is unacceptable and inexcusable is that embracement of the n-word is a mockery of Medgar Evers' death as well as the untold millions of enslaved African Americans who – as they drew their last breaths – would hear jeers of the n-word ringing in their ears.

Nonetheless, a multitude of excuses are advanced by those who use the word in a feeble attempt to justify their ill-advised actions. The truth of the matter is that the only true and authentic reason Blacks refer to one another as n**gas is because they are in denial of the fact that they are *mentally enslaved*, lost, confused and filled with a programmed self-hatred. The truth, no matter how cliché this may sound, can and will set them free; yet, they cannot handle the truth nor can the millions of non-users who condone use of the word by other Blacks. Many users of the n-word do so simply because they have been conditioned over centuries to use the word and now have no self-control over not using the word. Through and through, the n-word owns them *heart, mind, body* and *soul*.

There is no other word in the English language that encompasses such a tremendous wealth of negative power. Today, use of the word has been reduced to a racial slur, but it truly possesses the power to control the minds and actions of a race of people. This mind-controlling power is evident in that African American users are unable to tear themselves away from its clutches. Anything a person cannot live without *owns* and *controls* that individual thus making that person its slave.

The number one priority for the Black community should be an unconditional commitment to the *psychological* and *spiritual* liberation of all African Americans.
It begins with burying the n-word. As each Black African American consciously decides to increase his/her intellect—as enlightenment cannot be purchased—understands the ramifications of the term, and refuses to be referred to as such by friends, family, self, or anyone else, the Black community will progress unhindered. However, without this foundation of self-

respect, mental liberation and eventual *economic independence* will be impossible to achieve.

To be succinct, it all boils down to *mental* and *intestinal* fortitude. Take, for example, black actor Sidney Poitier. Others may have referred to him as an n-word, but he never allowed himself to succumb to the pressures of Jim Crowism, bigotry and biasness by being pressured into reducing himself to anything less than his own perception of his self-worth. Mr. Poitier was a mentally-liberated man and, therefore, did not kowtow to the established norms of society. By remaining dignified, honoring rather than desecrating his ancestry and heritage, or selling out the precious memories, struggles and sacrifices of his ascendants, he became a very successful, accomplished, and respected Hollywood actor.

For whatever reason, the black actors, actresses, and entertainers of today do not possess the mental and intestinal fortitude of a Sidney Poitier. Rather, acting like helpless and hopeless victims, relenting to an 18th century slave mentality of being someone's n**ga, they kowtow and submissively walk around hunched back walking like a duck refusing to stand up straight and take control of their own minds.

 It takes much courage, strength and guts to stand up to deracination.
Although it is far easier to submit to mental enslavement, *mentally-liberated black folks* do not acquiesce to being referred to as the n-word or desecrating the sacred memories of their ancestors. They elect to reverse and re-take control of their own minds.

One of the hardest things for people to be able to do is to really *think* and *act* for themselves. When it comes to the n-word African Americans have been conditioned to abide in a group-think environment which would explain their illogical embracing of the pejorative term along with those who may not personally use the term but will condone use of it from others. Little is taught about thinking for oneself, instead a lot of effort has been put forth by the American institutionalized systemic to solicit African Americans to think within a certain "frame of reference." However, if one dares to think outside of that frame, they are excoriated by those who are in compliance.

The benefits of clear thinking is that a person who can think effectively and *rationally* is more difficult to control. Thus institutions such as the music and movies industries are able to control people of color because of their irrational thinking and willingness to condescend to the level of infantile namby-pambies. Their embracing of the n-word weakens them to the point that almost everything they do ensures the destiny of their race to be control by others. The best way to counter-act mental enslavement is to learn how to think properly and reason things out so that one can have good information upon which to work, and above all else *grow up*. Selling one's soul to the devil for fortune and fame is a testimony of sickness and perversion and are not deserving of any exaltations and admirations.

Willpower is the key essence to breaking any sort of mental bondage. We all have it but some of us just lack focus and or the intestinal fortitude to overcome a given situation. Just as much as your subconscious can allow you to do things you aren't fully aware of sometimes, your conscious mind can also overcome just as well. Willpower is free and fully available to anyone and everyone who can handle it.

PART II

Three kinds of people exist in the world:

- ○ **Those who do what they're told without question**
- ○ **Those who control them**
- ○ **Those who refuse to play the game**

The third group is ENVIED AND HATED BY THE OTHER TWO.

Chapter 7

I am not European! Where is *my* history?

"A tree cannot stand without roots"
~Congolese Proverb

"History does not refer merely, or even principally, to the past. On the contrary, the great force of history comes from the fact that we carry it within us, are unconsciously controlled by it in many ways, and history is literally present in all that we do."
~James Baldwin

Baldwin's proclamation that *"the great force of history comes from the fact that we carry it within us"* is profound. He's saying, in other words, though attempts may be made to separate the past from the present, this feat is impossible as history is an integral and most prevalent living and evolving aspect in the foundation of the former, current, and future self. As such, history will constantly affect one's actions presently and in the future.

Black world and American history have been distorted; as a consequence, African Americans' collective self-confidence has been compromised because their founding cultures and personifying contributions to world civilization have been misshapen, erased, or forgotten. Sadly this fact is not atypical. In fact, efforts are constantly undertaken to veil the truth of Black American and world history from Black African Americans. Efforts are made to garble a remarkable history through distorting the facts and destroying physical evidence of a brilliant people to continue to oppress those same people. [6]

These attempts have been in play ever since the first enslaved African was delivered to the unknown land against their will. Since that day, up to present day, the truth about Black history—its heritage and culture—has been closely guarded and masked by their oppressors to ensure Black African Americans stay within their appointed place of being ignorant, detached so-called n**gers/n**gas.

George Orwell presents an argument in his novel, *1984*, which says that who controls the past controls the future, and who controls the present controls the past. All the books written about Blacks by their conquerors reflect the conquerors' viewpoints. Nothing else should have been expected. Considering how thoroughly captured were the minds of Blacks and the availability of *scholarly* materials on the market, it should be of no surprise—though it's no excuse either—that so many black scholars still faithfully follow in the footsteps of their white counterparts.

When applied to the teachings of American and world history, the mindset of many professional historians, authors of scholarly books in any arm of history, and "public" or politically-active intellectuals is often based in right-wing, conservative think tanks. The mass media epitomizes Orwellian aphorism; and henceforth, above all else, academia is used as a tool to *control* by any means necessary.

Clearly, Western civilization history is reflective of a perpetual continuity between the civilization of the Greeks and the Romans and that of the modern West. The history of Black Africa has been contemptuously dismissed as the unrewarding gyrations of barbarous tribes in picturesque but irrelevant corners of the globe.

Cultural wars and ideological struggles rage against interpretations of history that recognize the achievements of non-Western cultures. Influential historians support the view of Eurocentric history, which treats non-Western civilizations with contempt. However, critics of this ideology are looked upon as "Europhobes" who value *feeling* as compared to actually *knowing*; they are mistakenly painted with the broad stroke of promoting a globalist and multiculturalist agenda when in reality their only plight is to bring to view the notion that Europe is not the only continent to contribute to human civilization progress.

In line with the thinking of supposed "Europhobes," it is high time that not only Black America, but all of America and its many different races, realizes that all they are being *taught* is not the truth. The long-established Eurocentric history is subjective and outmoded in a rapidly-changing world where new questions inevitably arise; these questions callout the status quo and norms society has so long been conditioned to humbly accept. The old Western civilization course in history is tainted, outdated and has given students a misleading view of history. By misunderstanding history, these same students also possess inaccurate views of themselves in present day. Thus, to clear up this confusion, a reassessment of Black African American and world history is warranted.

History on every front has been communicated to the masses incorrectly. Caucasians worked very hard at trying to convince African Americans that they were athletically, culturally, and intellectually inferior to them. If this were true, why the need to try to brainwash Blacks into believing something that is supposedly a fact?

For instance, even with the unrelenting attempts of indoctrination, African Americans still seem to overcome and rise to the top athletically, culturally, and intellectually. In the world of sports: in 1908, Jack Johnson became the first black Heavyweight Champion of the World and reigned as champion until 1915. During the 1936 Olympics in Germany, Jesse Owens won four gold medals much to Hitler's consternation. Hitler, who had pronounced the white race as the Master Race, refused to shake Owens's hand unlike other gold medal winners. Joe Louis became heavyweight champion of the world in 1937, defeating Germany's title-holding Max Schmeling; Louis reigned as champ until 1949. Boxing and track & field exposed the myth of whites being athletically superior as a lie as black participants rose to dominate both sports.

In the realm of sports, this left baseball, basketball and football—the last major sports—for which to allow White America to attempt to keep the myth alive. Jackie Robinson became the first black man to play in the major leagues. Mr. Robinson was forced to overcome many incredible odds—not only proving physical ability, but most significantly, mental/emotional stamina and intestinal fortitude. In the wake of these trials, he prevailed, nonetheless, and opened the door for other black athletes to walk through. Robinson put to rest the mythical claims of white athletic superiority in that sport as well.

During the '50's, in order for Blacks to participate in sports at the high school level, they had to be twice as good as their white counterparts to make the team. While Whites thought their tough, unfair barriers to entry would discourage Blacks from participating, to the contrary, their challenge actually forced Blacks to run harder, think faster, and play more innovatively than their white teammates. This ultimately laid the groundwork for the emergence of black superstar athletes.

Next challenge: It has been assumed that Blacks do not have the intellectual ability to think for themselves or possess the capacity to lead. In all three major sports— basketball, football and baseball, the myth that Blacks lack the intellect to lead a team has been shattered. For instance, in football, black players were allowed to play every position with the exception of quarterback because they were supposedly not smart enough to play the position. African-American quarterback for the Washington Redskins Doug Williams' winning of the 1988 Super Bowl buried yet another myth.

NFL professional football was the last bastion to give way to the idea of Blacks' inability to and ineffectiveness at coaching when, in 2006, Tony Dungy of the Indianapolis Colts and Lovie Smith of the Chicago Bears simultaneously became the first black head coaches in a Super Bowl game.

Because of the highly-unmatched athletic capabilities of black people, many may believe that physical stamina and entertainment is Black America's only claim to fame. Barack Hussein Obama's election as the first inarguably black President of the United States of America completely demolished the myth that Blacks lack intelligence and the potential to lead. This phenomenal feat is an extraordinary accomplishment so much so that elements of White America flirted with the idea of eliminating the "One-drop Rule" of being Black.

The disastrous effects of the Eurocentric education system on Black Americans who, not having other frames of reference, have had to adopt the ideologies and viewpoints of Whites in order to survive, have been strong and evident. The American institutionalized systemic is set up to maintain the falsehood that Whites are intellectually superior to Blacks, and in order for this system to work, it's imperative that Blacks believe this themselves.

Unfortunately, an overwhelming number have adopted these mentalities and believe that Blacks are not as smart as Whites; their use of the n-word serves as validation. However, as further evidenced in the afore-mentioning of those who have attained truly remarkable, history-making feats that will progress society on a moral and conscious-awakening level, Black America does own the strength and tenacity to achieve and prevail. Even when the teachings and viewpoints were and still are against Black Americans from within and without the community, some Black Americans are able to mentally rise above the systemic and the internal brainwashing. They whole-heartedly refuse the negativity and falsehoods being preached to them, and make real strides for humankind in general.

Among other things, the solid black leadership and strong community activism that was prevalent during the '60's has since been neutralized. A mind control ploy that was somewhat dormant during that time also resurfaced: the n-word. The n-word—a significant element and lifeblood of the inferiority myths that run in full color throughout the Black community—is an ace card that America has used for more than 300 years as an effective tool to keep Black Americans mentally off-centered, off-balance and discombobulated.
The news media, an apparatus of the systemic, sends messages of self-destruction, self-abasement, complacency and inertia to Black Americans by way of black apostates, such as rappers, black comedians, and sycophant educators.

DR. CARTER G. WOODSON ONCE SAID: *"If you can make a man believe that he is inferior, you don't have to compel him to seek an inferior status, he will do so without being told."*

Dr. Carter G. Woodson
(1875 – 1950)

To constantly be told for more than three centuries that *your place* is that of a n**ger and that you *better never forget it* in of itself is reason enough –among a myriad of many others—for any African American to refrain from identifying with that word. Use of the term n**ga is nothing more than ghetto vernacular for n**ger and is a weak, feeble attempt at disguising the truth. Black America, as a group, voluntarily embracing their so-called appointed place as n**gers/n**gahs validates the resounding success of the *mental enslavement* indoctrination.

Black world history has been distorted and virtually obliterated, limiting it to the confines of the modern day habitat for a reason. Enough remaining evidence exists around the world to confirm that there was a very potent history surpassing that of life in the jungle and mud huts. Nonetheless, it is by design for Black African Americans not to know or understand anything about their past preceding the habitat from which Black ancestors were removed. [7]

Keeping Blacks detached from their past sits at the core of the systemic; if such a virus of knowledge is infused into the system, the entire beast will explode from the innermost parts to the tips of its furthest reaching tentacles. On such a day, African Americans will know real freedom...but because the systemic is mindful at even the notion of such a day, they work to secure Black America's place in the darkness at any cost. *At any cost!*

The myth of cultural inferiority fosters the idea that Blacks have never risen above life in the jungle or constructively contributed to the advancement of humankind. Evidence all around the world suggests the fallacy in this premise as well. For instance, when Napoleon invaded Egypt with his French army, he took offense to the Afroid features of the Sphinx's nose and ordered his troops to aim their cannon at the nose and blow it off.

Africa, once known as "The Land of the Blacks" was not only "The Cradle of Civilization" itself but it was home to the leading people on earth. Egypt, its true name "Kemet" and was derived by Blacks, was once inhabited by all black people. This society was comprised of pioneers in the sciences, medicine, architecture, writing, and the first builders who used stone as a key material in erecting buildings. Once *Kemet* became amalgamated with Asians mixing with Blacks, its name was changed to *Egypt*. [8]

The strong and established ancient civilizations of Blacks included Nubians, Ethiopians, Egyptians, Thebans, Libyans, Thinites, Cushites, Memphites, Numidians and others. However, when these kingdoms fell upon their dark periods, all were invaded by barbarians from the north with the exception of Nubia Kush. Only Nubia Kush remained powerful until the

1500's when Arab invaders infiltrated and began enslaving Blacks. The invaders are still there today.

Over the past four hundred years, racist theories have been concocted to justify the enslavement and colonization of Blacks on a worldwide scale. Yet, from the 1600's and dating as far back as 15,000 years prior to that period, Black civilization was the most dominant and advanced on earth. It is important to understand and know that the though the main focus is generally on Egypt, the tentacles of thriving Black civilizations reached throughout the continent of Africa.

From the time of the Roman conquest of Europe from about 400 B.C. to around 1200 A.D., much of Northern and Western Europe was in a stage of barbarism and backwardness. The Roman settlements and cities built by the Romans were the only areas of advanced culture.

Around 711 A.D. when the Moors, a Black people from Senegal, West Africa and Morocco, invaded Europe, they introduced science, technology, Black Moorish civilization and education to Europe. The Moors raised the Europeans out of the Dark Ages. The Black Moors introduced advanced learning to Spain, similar to what had been taking place in Ghana and at the university city of Jenne in Mali for hundreds of years.
They introduced advanced learning to the cities of Toledo, Seville and Cordoba. These cities became centers of Black Moorish and European scholarship, science and culture, where Europeans and others learned new and advanced sciences, arts and technologies. That led to the European Renaissance of later years. The Black Moors introduced art, architecture, sciences, medicines, animal husbandry and other advanced disciplines to Spain and the rest of Europe. This was the catalyst which led to the European Renaissance.[9]

Relative to American history, John Horse's name is conveniently omitted from the pages of American history; even still, it is a name in which all Black African Americans should be familiar. Horse was an African-American military adviser to Chief Osceola and a leader of Black Seminole units fighting against United States troops during the Seminole Wars in Florida. Of Seminole-African-Spanish descent, he moved to Indian Territory (present day Oklahoma) during the Indian Removal in 1842 and was personally freed in 1843. When the Black Seminoles faced continuing threats from slave raiders, he led a group to northern Mexico, where they attained freedom in 1850. Horse served as a captain in the Mexican army and, after 1870, with the US Army as a scout.[10]

As well, General Toussaint L'Ouverture, the leader of a Haitian slave revolt, defeated the superpower British army and Napoleon's French army. However, Eurocentric historical references to such events are generally and conveniently overlooked.

Whites and Arabs alike have conspired to wipe out virtually any and all traces of thriving Black civilizations and their contributions to humankind. To what lengths are men prepared to continue allowing prejudice, bias and racism to misrepresent the truth? More importantly, why *even* the *need* for misrepresentation? Why the need to keep a race of people in the dark about their past? What secrets lay hidden in the Black race's past that are only known by the Arab nation and those of Euro-centricity that are so important to keep from Blacks? Are the powers to be fearful that *when* African Americans do finally wake up and learn about their history that they will find such great strength, fortitude, and direction that they may realize their worth and rise to heights of greatness once before obtained millenniums ago? [11]

One may also ask how highly-advanced Black civilizations were so completely destroyed that its people, in current times and for some centuries past, have found themselves not only behind the other groups of the world economically, but also lacking in self-awareness and pride? How is it that the once prideful people now believe that the color of their skin is a sign of inferiority, bad luck, and the badge of the slave whether bound or free? Africa was initially under siege by the Arabs followed centuries later by a European invasion. Over a period of time, some Blacks trying to escape the invasion of their war-torn lands and the capture and enslavement of their peoples fled to the remotest parts of the continent. As a consequence, they regressed in culture. [12]

Harsh environments, isolation and the lack of resources contributed to the then current generation's inability to develop at the same level of the vast majority of other African and Black kingdoms, states, empires and societies of their time. The cataclysm has been used by racists to classify the Black race as "undeveloped." Thus, all Black culture and civilizations are placed into the same category as those who were isolated and eventually regressed from being once great people. Slavery, colonialism and oppression were the final blows that contributed to the retardation of great Black African civilizations.

Moreover, the introduction of gunpowder to Europe from China via the Arabs played a major part in elevating the Europeans to a level of military superiority. This advantage over Africans made colonialism and the theft of African lands as well as the defeat of some African armies easier than in past eras. When the Europeans fought with sword and lance against sword and lance, their victories against Africans were few.

For example, Hannibal, the African from Carthage, defeated Rome's legions with as little as 15,000 men and ruled Italy for many years.

However, even with contemporary weapons during the modern era, Europeans were sometimes soundly defeated. Nations such as the Zulus, Mossi States, Ashanti, Dahomians, Ethiopians and others defeated the Europeans in a number of wars and battles. Eventually, the use of better, more effective weaponry by the Europeans was one of the determining factors that enabled them to conqueror Africa. Weapons of sorts were Europeans' separating factors from the rest of the races. These same weapons, along with religion, keep Blacks and others oppressed to this very day, rather than any innate "superiority" aspect.

In other words, the other contributing factor or weapon that permitted Europeans to take control, was their political and manipulative use of *religion*. The pairing of guns and self-serving use of religion has proven to be a formidable and potent combination in propelling Europeans to the status of a "ruling class." The American motto is *In God We Trust.* However, in practice God ranks third behind: 1) The Almighty Dollar and 2) Firearms, then comes 3) God.

For those who are seekers of the truth, no matter the color of one's skin, the story of how such an advanced civilization has been virtually eliminated from the annals of history—and how use of religion became a significant ploy—is one of the greatest and most tragic in the history of humankind. This *history* or occurrence of events should be the main focus of research studies in Black African history.

A generation of Black scholars convey the doctrines and viewpoints of their white counterparts like so many robots without minds of their own. By corroborating, they have the blessings of academia and are not smeared. On the other hand, Black historian scholars who are independent thinkers and having proved to have mental and intestinal fortitude are portrayed as having the incapacity to deal with African history objectively; thus, their Black history textbooks are not readily available, but with some effort, are obtainable.

At the 1974 Cairo Symposium, full professors of Egyptology meet to challenge the findings of black historians and scholars. Among them, black scholars Dr. Cheikh Anta Diop and Dr. Theophile Obenga were tasked with presenting their findings and proving the validity of the findings. By the end of the symposium, Dr. Diop and Dr. Obenga had scientifically proven their case that ancient Egyptians were indeed black; subsequently, the general consensus reached at the Symposium was that no evidence existed to support the notion that the ancient Egyptians were white. The UNESCO's "General History of Africa" meeting minutes of the 1974 Cairo Symposium validates the scientific evidence presented by Cheikh Anta Diop and Theophile Obenga.

On another occasion, professors of Egyptology met to once again challenge the findings of black historians and scholars. This event took place at a Temple University Conference. The evidence was so overwhelming in favor of black historians that professors of Egyptology have since refrained from challenging the findings.

These findings, discovered and proven by black people, of course brought on many avalanches of assaults that were soon to follow. During the 1980's and '90's, black historians supportive of African studies found themselves being character assassinated and smeared as shams and con artists by White American and British scholars; in some instances, they were even interrogated by other black scholars.

Eric Martel, a white high school teacher in Washington, D.C., wrote to thousands of schools in the United States condemning Afrocentricity. In his letter, he listed a number of black historians and scholars whose publications he felt teachers and administrators should remove from their classroom libraries; in other words, Black Americans and no one else should have access to the works. That is the act of an autocratic person and unwarranted censorship.

During the late '80's, every major newspaper, magazine, and journal as well as countless radio and television talk shows engaged in a unilateral assault against Afrocentricity. These attacks lasted throughout the '90's. Several books were written attacking Afrocentricity, some of which alluded to such claims that certain black scholars were pulling the nation apart by the mere fact that African traditions were being studied. Some of the books written were *The Disuniting of America* by Arthur Schlesinger; *Not Out of Africa* by Mary Lefkowitz, which challenges the fundamental notion that Africans *are* Africans; *Afrocentrism Mythical Path and Imagined Homes* by Oxford scholar Steven Howell; *The End of Racism* by Dinesh D'Souza, arguing that racism does not exist in America.

Black Athena Revisited by Mary R. Lefkowitz; *Alternatives to Afrocentrism* by Linda Chavez; and *Closing of the American Mind* by Alan Bloom, which prompted college and university administrators all around the country to hold meetings to discuss the dismantling of African-American studies.

Bell Curve by Charles Murray was also one that was published during this time. The book argues that Blacks are genetically inferior to white people. The author's publishing funds were provided by the Olin Foundation and the American Enterprise Institute.

When black scholars appeared before the full professors of Egyptology, they presented their case with hard core scientific facts which could not be refuted. It should be made clear that when black scholars were arguing their points, it was not that the teaching of Western civilization itself was under attack, but the fundamental *exclusions* and *misrepresentations* of African civilizations were the cause for speculation and discussion. Yet, even in knowing this, assaults were still launched against these black scholars by people lacking the proper credentials and understanding to even speak on such a topic; rather, their frustrations were only really based upon characterization of the works and attacking the authors of such works.

Strategically, there were no engaging, disputing, recording and/or challenging documentation against the facts and notions presented in the scholars' works. The fact is that African studies destroy the myth of Western civilization, and those under the spell will go to any and great lengths to keep the voice of Black America smothered to hear only the wailing cry of white supremacy.

Worthy to note, black historians and scholars do have some white support. This support includes historians such as Gerald Massey; Basil Davison; Joel Freeman; scientist Richard Neave; and archeologist, anthropologist Walter Neves, to name a few. It would be a degradation of African history and unacceptable if the present system of racial lies embedded in world literature was destroyed only to replace it with glorified fiction based more on wishful thinking and feelings than on the labors of historical research. [13]

Black scholars such as Dr. John Henri Clarke, Dr. Chancellor Williams, Dr. Amos Wilson, Dr. Cheikh Anta Diop, Dr. Asa Hilliard, Dr. Carter G. Woodson, and

George G.M. James, just to name a few, are more than worthy of attention. These scholars actually worked in the field (real life), many living during the turn of the times (lawful end of slavery).

They conducted primary research to see for themselves the state of Black America, to detect its causes of demise and offer valid solutions to resolution. Although this is by no means a complete list of all the real history makers, it is an excellent starting point, qualified sample and representation of honorable and trustworthy people who committed and devoted their lives to researching the truth relative to Black African history.

Unfortunately, few may know of these men, and truth be told, this veiling was intended by systemic design. At the end of this book, however, will be a list of suggested readings containing some of those high-achieving men's works along with others. Every Black American should be as equally familiar with these co-architects of the American nation as many are with such names as George Washington, Benjamin Franklin, and Thomas Jefferson.

Enlightenment and knowledge of one's past history is an important and necessary step toward *mental liberation* and the ability to proceed forward in a positive and constructive fashion. One cannot be whole without knowing their origins. As the old adage goes, *you can't know where you are going if you don't know where you have been.* One cannot comfortably relate to others if that person does not know who they are; thus, if one cannot naturally and genuinely relate to others, it becomes difficult to feel positive about self. This phenomenon helps to explain the low self-esteem and mis-direction among so many black people.

To understand and appreciate one's history is to understand self. In understanding self, it allows the group that individual is born of to gradually open the window to ingenuity and inner creativity. Though the individual achievements in Black America cannot be denied, *unified group* accomplishments remain stagnant in Black modern day society. If the community is to excel beyond its current situation, *collective progress* will be required.

The truth can lie dormant and/or be concealed for millenniums and yet find a way to re-emerge and reveal its unabridged reality. However, continued inertia assures an infinite span of *mental enslavement* for the Black race. Self-internalizing and perpetual use of the n-word serves as a psychological conduit for this type of bondage. It remains to be seen as to how much longer Black America—as a group—will continue to allow itself to be victimized, bamboozled and hoodwinked into acceptance of an 18th century slave mentality.

It behooves self-respecting Blacks to re-claim their rightful and dignified place in history; otherwise, the race will remain irrelevant and presented as inferior useless beings taking up valuable space in the pages of ancient history. The silent majority must take a look in the mirror and say: "Let it begin with me! And let me not rest until I have helped my community once again stand as a strong, viable, and united people." There has to be a revolution, but it *has* to be a revolution of

consciousness.

Black people have a history so glorious that slavery is nothing more than a by-product of a fall from grace. The main problem lies in the fact that even when physical bondage ended and the Black race was supposed to again re-claim their rightful place, they lacked the energy, spirit, and wanting desire to do so.

Even though the great ones are challenged and may even fall, the true strength in being great is derived in the ability to willingly rise again in the face of short-term or seeming defeat. Oppressors realize this cycle, but would rather for the Black race to continue feeling beat down, or defeated, and to think of slavery as their only contribution to humankind. This sense of brokenness and helplessness is exactly what the oppressors planned and banked on.

Oppressors prefer for African Americans to focus on the negative period of their history hoping they will remain so pre-occupied with being stressed, depressed and regressed with slavery that they will continue to overlook, downplay, or completely remain ignorant to the many thousands of years of greatness, unity, African love and innovation in which they once basked. One thing they did not bet on is Black America re-gaining an unwavering sense of togetherness and strength that was displayed during the 60s. That enduring spirit and tangible greatness can again be attained if Black America is willing to accept its heritage in totality and re-connect to its life source of a rich and abundant history and lose the 18th century slave mentality of being a n**ga.

Carter G. Woodson, in his book, *The Mis-Education of the Negro*, wrote:

> "WE SAY HOLD ON TO THE REAL FACTS OF HISTORY AS THEY ARE, BUT COMPLETE SUCH KNOWLEDGE BY STUDYING ALSO THE HISTORY OF RACES AND NATIONS WHICH HAVE BEEN PURPOSELY IGNORED. WE SHOULD NOT UNDERRATE THE ACHIEVEMENTS OF MESOPOTAMIA, GREECE AND ROME; BUT WE SHOULD GIVE EQUALLY AS MUCH ATTENTION TO THE INTERNAL AFRICAN KINGDOMS, THE SONGHAY EMPIRE AND ETHIOPIA, WHICH THROUGH EGYPT

DECIDEDLY INFLUENCED THE CIVILIZATION OF THE
MEDITERRANEAN WORLD."

With all of the available black scholars and historians, it is unfathomable how the group does not take the initiative to set the record straight regarding the true history of the Black civilization. Far too many Blacks, and Whites for that matter, are left with the impression that Blacks have never contributed anything to civilization and that the legacy primarily is limited to enslavement and a jungle habitat. For Black African Americans to allow themselves to be intimidated into thinking such falsehoods are true serves as validation of paternalistic and enslaved minds lacking the ability and desire to want to think for self, but then again it does earn one the right to sit on the highest court in the land, the Supreme Court.

Many already own the skills/know-how and desire to occupy a firm footing in the new-world reality. The issue lies in African Americans' seeming inability to overcome the paternalistic attitudes that were so long ago embedded into them before birth. If Blacks are to become "qualified" for their rightful positions, re-forming of mentalities into that of a higher-thinking, higher self-respecting race must occur straightaway. Moreover, by ascending the mind to a greater mind power, any lacking skills will be intuitively sought and attained.

The first step toward proof that this transformation is occurring will be the eradication of the n-word from the vocabulary and intellectual dictionaries. One proud Black African American has already taken this step: Attorney Roy Miller was successful in having the n-word removed from a major dictionary. Once this label is peeled from the psyche, Black America will then be able to see itself as, act as, and reap the deserving benefits of equal, non-categorized, qualified people.

For every ONE African who actually lived through the torture of enslavement, TEN died. Black Americans are the children of African ancestors who were the strongest and best of those who were stolen from the Motherland. As such, hark on Mother-Father Africa. Study about places like ancient Mali, Songhai, Ghana and discover that this world would not be what it is if the Black race did not have the capabilities, dedication and love needed in order to work together for common causes, goals and the good of a people... Bring it back, and say: "Let it begin with me!"

The Odyssey of Haiti

At a moment in time, Haiti was the richest and most prosperous colony in the Americas. So what happened? Pat Robertson, the American Christian televangelist and host of "The 700 Club", attributes Haiti's misfortunes—in light of a 7.0 earthquake that shook the island-nation—to the nation having a sworn pact with the devil.

Robertson states:

> *[Hatians] were under the heel of the French...and they got together and swore a pact to the devil. They said, 'We will serve you if you will get us free from the French.' True story. And so the devil said, 'Ok it's a deal.' And they   kicked the French out. The Haitians revolted and got themselves free, but ever since they have been cursed by one thing after another.*

Of course native Haitians did defeat Napoleon and the French colonists in 1804 to declare their independence; however, Robertson's innuendoes and half-truths about Haiti's deteriorating social, political and economic conditions are just that—half-truths.

Something did indeed happen a long time ago and Robertson is correct in saying that people might not—and generally do not—talk about it, but not for the reasons he implies.

What people do not openly talk about is the black Haitian rebel leader General Toussaint L'Ouverture. No one discusses that fact that L'Ouverture not only defeated Napoleon and the French army, but prior to that and after a five-year war, the general defeated world super-power Great Britain. This victory for Haiti classified the Haitian's War of Independence as the world's first historical, successful slave revolution.

To make sure the contagion and news of the Haitian's success did not spread to the United States and Latin America where scores of slaves salivated over freedom and were willing to take life or death risks to obtain it, an international blockade occurred. The island was isolated and quarantined. The Haitians were left on their own to survive, and to add insult to injury, found themselves having to pay reparations to the French as opposed to receiving it themselves. This in-debtedness subsequently led to the dire and dismal conditions of this island, leaving it—to this very day—in a constant impoverished state.

After the French defeat, Napoleon—through deception and false pretense—summoned General Toussaint L'Ouverture to France where he was immediately arrested and imprisoned. Haiti was left leaderless, and, thus, left to fend for itself with no guidance: cut the head off a snake or the roots from a tree, and the rest of the body will wither and die. Since that point in time, corruption, bigotry, and poverty have reigned over the country.

In considering this current event, Pat Robertson's "confession," and the afore-mentioned brief history lesson, the reader must be reminded that there is and always has been a truth-problem and sharing bias in America. Rightly, although it is absolutely necessary to continually acknowledge and share the truth, the discussion must offer real, unbiased truth of accounts in every situation/event regardless to one's feeling of the matter or fears of the effects such a "truth" may cause.

Along this same line of discussion, it is of great necessity that truth-sharing (knowledge-sharing) occur among individuals throughout the Black race. Without Blacks taking accountability for sharing Black History and African American studies in colleges and universities, the Black community will remain audience to devices with a favorable Eurocentric spin on all and everything that took place in the past. If black people do not know their own history, the race of people will be left at the hands of these Eurocentric ideals that continue to preach inferiority and indignity about black people on the whole.

Traditional African institutions must be isolated from those later influenced by Islamic Arabs and Christian Europe. Only in this way can Black America determine what the Black heritage truly represented. Instead of just talking about "identity", black people shall know at last precisely the purely-African body of principles, value systems or philosophies of life that gradually evolved from forefathers over countless ages. From securing this perfect understanding, a new, real and feasible African ideology can be developed to effectively guide the Black race directly toward its truest potential.

Concisely, no real unanimity to Black heritage can be attained until the true heritage is known. All of the answers are hidden in the broken, misshapen, and obscure history. The Black race has been drifting along, wallowing blissfully in the cordial heritage of other people. This ignorance, detachment, and confusion must end today.

Remember, that *who* you are is limited only by who you *think* you are; and who *you think you are* is founded on the knowledge of who *you know you are*. How abundant or deficient this knowledge fortress is will be reflected in self-awareness—complete understanding of *self*, self-confidence, and the ability to identify and separate truth from lies. One cannot be whole without knowing who they are—their roots, heritage, and history. Activities and studies must reach beyond the limit of educating Blacks on just Eurocentric American and World History, and span the seas, shores, and time to include all occurrences that have touched the life of any dark-skinned person or people from Africa.

Proverbs 29:18, *"Where there is no vision, the people perish."* Self-knowledge serves as a compass to vision. Without it, one is likened to a sailboat without sails simply foundering aimlessly in the ocean of life.

Chapter 8

Group vs Individual Successes

Collective progress—the by-product of racial unity and the key to the Black race's advancement and longevity

"If you want to go quickly, go alone. If you want to go far,
Go Together"
~African Proverb

In spite of the numerous blatant and subliminal social obstacles that the Black community has faced in the past and continues to face, over the last 100 years, a remarkable number of African Americans have risen to highly-esteemed statuses in the professions, arts, letters, professional sports and the entertainment field. Within the past 15 years, two Black Secretaries of State have held office, a few Black U.S. Senators and governors have been elected to serve, and the first acknowledged Black president has earned a seat in the oval office. Each of these individuals' accomplishments and many more by other African Americans has seemingly helped Black America to progress significantly since the 1960's.

However, when Black America is placed under a microscope, a malignant picture emerges. Though much individual success has occurred sporadically among Blacks, *virtually* no group achievement prevails. Black America is divided and fragmented, and comes in last place in relation to other races in terms of group or collective progress.

Minority groups such as Asians, Hispanics, and Jews are far more productive. Their communal success can be attributed to their "greater good" mentality and their willingness to stand united; re-distribute their income within their communities to build and strengthen their communities; as well as assist one another in their individual plights toward success by sharing knowledge, skills, and access to resources. The communal help will ultimately uplift their entire society.

Contrarily, the concept of unity and community is foreign to Black African Americans; seemingly, the thinking that prevails within the Black community is the "crabs in a bucket" mentality. Rather than linking hands with one another and building ladders to help others climb to the top to attain success and take the Black community to the next greatest level, every man seeks their own personal gain or wealth. They crawl over one another or outright sacrifice the lives and psyche of others within their community to gain a dollar.

This fact is most apparent in rappers degrading black women and promoting ignorance to the masses of black youth; hustlers selling drugs on the corner and aspiring only to becoming the neighborhood king pen; entertainers consistently using the n-word for laughs; and communities failing to participate in or create social movements to benefit the Black race collectively.

Worthy to note and interestingly enough, present day Black Americans tend to disassociate with native Africans. Black Americans tend to feel that they are superior to immigrant Africans. However, migrant Africans who voluntarily migrated to America from Africa tend to follow a strong communal effort in helping one another become established and create a good life for themselves. Black Americans laugh at them, but it seems that African Americans from Africa come to America and actually take a larger slice of the American dream that Black Americans are entitled to by the hard work of their forefathers. The foreign African Americans seem to be mitigated from the effects of American slavery and operate on a free mentality versus a bonded slave mentality so many

American-born Blacks fashion. As such, it would do Black Americans some good to learn from their *real* brethren.

When will African Americans realize that until the Black community unites from within and makes strides as a group, no African American will be able to experience the true fullness of freedom, respect and equality? Even President Obama is often times racially disrespected (i.e., the "Baby Monkey" email shenanigans) and referenced as the n-word. Until Blacks unite as one and respect one another from within the group, respect from without is never, ever going to become a reality.

New York Post caricature of President Obama

Malcolm X once said, "[w]e cannot think of becoming acceptable unto others until we have first become acceptable to ourselves." When looking at the Black community, the capital income exceeds that of most third world countries. Yet, only about 5% of that capital remains in the community. It is projected that by year 2015, the Black community's spending power will exceed a trillion dollars.

Sadly, everyone else benefits from African Americans' capital gains except African Americans. Something psychologically wrong exists with the way many African Americans think. If one's very own community is not important enough for one to invest in financially and morally, how can Blacks really expect others to provide and care about the race? Consider the fact that Kobe Bryant, Los Angeles Lakers' NBA superstar, was once fined $100,000 for using the derogatory slur "faggot" towards a referee. The fine illustrates the NBA's zero tolerance for use of a derogatory term. However, when it comes to black players' use of the n-word, the NBA policy has been to look the other way. Is this because of the Black community's passive and submissive attitude relative to the use of the n-word amongst themselves?

It does not cost one red cent for African Americans to free themselves from the psychological bondage of the n-word, inferior thinking, and self-destructive behaviors; yet, Blacks as a group do not want to put forth the effort to take back their rightful dignity and self-respect that so freely and eagerly awaits their pick up. So why do African Americans insist on making fools of themselves and forfeiting any possibility at unity and collective progression by publicly degrading their own race?

Public use of the n-word by black users does absolutely nothing to elevate or uplift the image of the Black African American. Jewish people would never publicly refer to one another as *kike* or *Hymie*, the gay community publicly to each other as *faggots*, or Hispanics to one another as *wetbacks* or *spics*. So why do Black African Americans stoop so low and go to great lengths to disgrace, dishonor and bring contempt upon themselves by insisting on residing in their pre-appointed so-called place as a n**ga/n**ger? Have they been *that* brainwashed? The answer: an unequivocal *yes!* Certainly, the rest of the world watches in utter amazement and shock as African Americans dog and totally disrespect each other.

The n-word is a derogatory term no matter whose mouth it flows from, black or non-black. The n-word is a term that by its very intent was meant to engender separatism and brokenness. Before any race can progress forward, it must first be unified from within to not only withstand the many assaults that will be hurled at the group but to also make substantial and impacting strides that will define a new level or standard of achievement for all in the group.

Yet, if the group cannot even get on the same page within its own community, any form of substantial group progression will be impossible. Similar to building a fence: if only certain planks or sections of the fence are tightly adhered to the posts, when the builder goes to stand it up, the other end of the fence may fall, waffle, have a huge slouch or wave in it. The deformity will prevent the fence from serving its purpose. However, if each individual plank is steadfastly secured to the posts, when it is time to put the fence up, it will be erected without a problem. The fence, by design, will stand strongly against the elements and predators for an indefinite period of time.

Since the days of Malcolm X and Martin Luther King, Jr., Black America has been devoid of significant leadership. During the 1960's, African Americans as a group had a sense of pride, dignity and self-respect, but that has since eroded from the collective community. As a collective group, Blacks hold the key to turn things around, but they must realize it is a conscious choice to unite and do so.

Black America must understand the game that has been played on the group—as a whole—and *accept* the fact that the n-word, n**ger/ n**ga, is the lifeline that feeds the on-going cultural genocide. Some say that there are more important or prevalent issues occurring in the Black community than worrying about the use of the n-word. To that statement, the question is raised: what if the *cause* of all of those highly-significant and more pressing issues tied directly back to a *"smaller, seemingly less important"* factor—the n-word?

To paint a clearer picture: use of the n-word can be thought of as a single cell of bacteria that invades the body. It starts out as a small thing—say a small cough, aching muscles or limited use/range of motion, or blotch on the skin. However, given time, those same minor bacterial cells can morph into diseases that end up severely sickening (ie, pneumonia), crippling (ie, polio) and even killing (ie, AIDS, cancer, etc.) the host. The n-word as *just a "small" word* has this same type of effect—psychologically.

Realistically, if all Black Americans were to stop using the n-word overnight, surely change would not occur immediately; however, that would begin planting the seed of change and showing all within and without the Black community that Blacks are serious about themselves *once* again. The change can very well take two or three generations to overcome a 400-year-old slave habit. During this transitioning time, a foundation of self-respect must be established, which will necessarily include cold-turkey breaking the habit of referring to one another as the n-word. That would be the first and right step in that direction.

Group preservation, the primal instinct or natural desire to protect self and stay alive, is a universal, normal and natural phenomenon for all living organisms. In the event of a perceived threat, the life form settles into survival mode and begins to exhibit those behaviors that ensure the organism's existence. However, human beings' ability to self-protect is far superior to that of the basic organism's "fight or flight"- only option. Humans have a brain capable of perceiving and solving problems. People have the ability to consciously respond to or alter the response to a stimulus.

Group preservation is a coping mechanism one needs to prevent emotional trauma from distorting the mind and adversely affecting one's mentality. It seems as though all groups—regardless of race, creed and nationality, if felt threatened, would follow their survival instincts: these groups have the ability to think beyond the basic, primal level of individual survival and use their leverage—the human brain—to ensure their on-going protection and existence. They identify the threat and appropriately respond to it in a way that allows them to not only physically survive, but to smartly organize themselves and collectively strategize on ways of ensuring the problem's suppression to make sure it has no long-term implications on their "pack."

Not since the 1960's Civil Rights Movement have the African-American group exhibited these same types of superior, group survival demeanors. Today's African Americans have been conditioned to distance themselves from their collective group. They are either in denial or just simply despise their race.

The lost souls are uncertain of what, or even why, they are denying or despising their cultural truth; the worst part, however, is that even in spite of this overwhelming deficit, they still care not to identify the reasoning behind or damaging ramifications of the particular feeling of separation. The notion or concept of a collective identity is totally foreign or ludicrous to many Blacks, and whenever any attempt to enlighten is made, some quickly brand these attempts as evil, racist and non-productive.

Unfortunately, large pockets of Blacks feel that anything black is inferior and anything white, superior; they adopt a mindset that "if you are black, stay back; if you are white, you are right." These brainwashed African Americans have abandoned their community under the false pretense of supporting a post-racial society. It would be altruistic if all could simply be acknowledged and looked upon as just being "an American" without any reference to one's race. In that type of ideal utopian world, the post-racial position would be believable and possible.

However, this is America, a country that once blatantly accepted the idea that the oppressed people exist only for the good of the oppressor; one that worked relentlessly to keep Blacks separated and detached from their roots—for these oppressors know the power in cultural unity and collective identity.

Further, if all Americans were treated as first class citizens and acknowledged as such, there would be no need for the passing of any civil rights bills or laws. As such, trading collective preservation at the race or cultural group level for a post-racial stand is not logical, seems quite delusional, and perpetuates the idea of keeping Blacks—and any other oppressed group— broken and separated rather than united and powerful.

Petty differences must be set aside. For once, the African-American community must band together in efforts to heighten African-American values and standards, take charge of their own destiny, and stop serving as a doormat for the rest of the world.

The initial step is for African Americans to stop blindly accepting and defining themselves—a beautiful, intelligent, self-actualizing people—with a racist definition that stands for everything contrary to the African-American ethnic group. Underestimating the necessity of eliminating the n-word from all people's vocabulary is sheer folly, and would be a mistake with catastrophic ramifications for all.

Particularly for Black America, if the race of people is to experience rejuvenation and cultural strength, the group must realize the significance of collective progress. Once the community begins to think on one accord, each of the individual members or individual contributions will begin to mesh together, growing at an exponential weight to eventually become a walking, unstoppable giant. However, the first step is in establishing racial unity; that unity can only be found in removing all things that preach and promote separatism in the Black community, including the n-word.

Other factors limiting Black collective progress: Black Americans an endangered species?

Life is a struggle and only the mentally and physically strong survive. In a Comedy Central TV special, comedian DL Hughley lobbies the EPA to have Black African-American males declared an endangered species. Although DL Hughley's "The Endangered List" reduces the severe possibility of the Black man's impeding extinction to a comedy skit, this is a very serious and weighty matter.

The problem with attempting to bring attention to substantial issues using comedy is that the issue will be taken as a joke, fall upon deaf ears and blown off nonchalantly as a fictitious story made up just for kicks.

As such, those at the crux of the joke—Black America in totality—will also be taken as a joke. Hughley's approach is reminiscent of White America's belief that black people are light-hearted fools who are happy with the current status quo.

Many contributing factors lend to the very real possibility of Black American males becoming extinct. Some of the primary factors include Black-on-Black crime that ends all too often in tremendous amounts of bloodshed and death or life-long prison sentences; mediocre to poor health due to unhealthy eating habits; carelessness about or a reactive (rather than a proactive) nature toward tending to one's health; self-destructive, reckless lifestyle behaviors; and having no or limited access to medical care. Other situations that will effectively sponsor this sad affair include women using abortions as a form of birth control—which further leads to increased reproductive and mental issues; rampant drug abuse throughout the entire race; and same sex marriages. All of these issues are bound to have an adverse effect on population growth.

Speaking of population, grippingly, the United States holds less than five percent of the world's population, but it possesses almost a quarter of the world's prisoners. Interestingly, America is supposed to be the most civilized and organized country in the world, operating under the premise of the so-called justice system, yet America's prison population is the largest in the world.

A number of statistics are available breaking down the composition of the prison population, and a few particularly stand out: the prison population grew by 700 percent from 1970 to 2005. According to the 2010 census and Bureau of Justice Statistics (BJS), Blacks comprised 13.6% of the US population, yet accounted for 39.4% of the total prison and jail population in 2009.

Statistics further dictate that one in every 15 Black African-American men are currently incarcerated, and that, at a minimum, one in every three Black men can expect to go to prison at some point in their lifetime. As for other races, only one in every 106 white males is incarcerated, and one in every 36 for Hispanic males is locked up. The prison industry is big business.

Young men of color have a disproportionate number of encounters with law enforcement, indicating that racial profiling continues to be a problem. This is just one example of White America feeling like it has an unmoving commitment to fulfill its quota of incarcerating young black men. Do not be deluded about it, the prison cells will be filled by any means necessary.

A report by the Department of Justice found that Blacks and Hispanics were approximately three times more likely to be searched during a traffic stop than white motorists. African Americans were twice as likely to be arrested and almost four times as likely to experience the use of force during encounters with the police.

When considering all the emotional stress and the effects it has on the human mind and body, little wonder that young black males have the shortest life span of any group in America—another factor contributing to the group's human extinction.
Add abortions into the mix and the odds of extinction increase exponentially. Black America accounts for roughly 13% of the population and has 37% of the abortions. Eighty percent of Planned Parenthoods are located in minority neighborhoods, and the purpose of its existence is controversial to say the very least.

Founder Margaret Sanger's belief and acceptance of eugenics has given her the reputation of advocating Black genocide.

One thing is certain: an extermination of black babies is taking place, and Planned Parenthood is right in the midst of it all.

So, why these statistics? Why do "*experts*" speculate and actively pursue this type of continual demise for the Black community? How is that not only does the black man make up more than a third of the current prison population, but even greater, more negative predictions for disaster are made about him before he can even set foot to make a mistake? And if current trends continue the way they have been going, why is it that in the face of this type of report and revolting expectation, Black America continues to lead ill-fated, self-deprecating lives?

To be succinct, causes leading up to the black man's ill-fated situation does not strictly hinge on issues of poverty, unemployment, and drug abuse, all of which are prevailing concerns in the Black community. Rather, these factors are symptoms, not the cause; and these symptoms have heavily contributed to the state of Black America. Even further, though, Black America continues to lean on the systemic crutch as an excuse for allowing these symptoms to uncontrollably plague the community, which too, must be addressed.

Rather than Black America continuing to fall like marching soldiers over a cliff head first into the lifestyles that have been handed them by a system meant to destroy the race, Black America—especially the black men who are supposed to be the leaders of the community—must come to their senses and find methodical and strategic ways to circumnavigate this detrimental landscape. It is up to Black America to lasso the chaos as much as possible to make sure Black America sups its full portion of life's glories even though the cards were never dealt favorably for Black African Americans.

In many ways, the Black American male is thriving (*socially and economically*) as he never has before. Even still, he faces, at the same time, an assortment of conditions. These conditions, experts say, indicate that the species "is definitely threatened" and possibly endangered. This threat of extinction is real, and, yes, Black America to some extent must now accept responsibility for its own demise.

Black African Americans are the only group on earth who do not think in terms of *group* survival, although the much-needed group survival instincts were alive in the '60's. Now, totally consumed by individual successes and *"getting my own,"* Black America has allowed itself to be blinded by the entrapment of integration which has obliterated all instincts for group survival.

Moreover, many within the Black community are delusional as a result of 400 years of mind control. With all the happenings in the world today, it is not impractical to believe that the Black community is doubly oppressed. On top of the Black community dealing with needing to break away from 400 years of mental enslavement, with the threat of a class-war, the American government has seemingly begun to devise strategies of chipping away ALL Americans' civil liberties.

The further reduction of civil liberties will lead to withholding even more of Black Americans' freedoms. Making no excuses, this dual dilemma could be another solid contributing factor to the disillusionment and confusion that runs rampantly throughout the Black community.

At any rate, though, Black America must decide that extinction will not be a truth, move from living in captivity—mentally and physically in jails and prisons, and turn attention and real effort to fixing the root causes rather than wallowing in the symptoms. Black Americans are the only ones who can solidly work toward re-establishing itself as a pure and unified race who refuses to be wiped away from God's green earth by self, man or any man-made force.

A good place to start this re-unification process is in the pursuit of self-respect and respecting each other. Referring to one another as n**ga/n**ger is not a sign of respect but that of self-hatred, contempt and acceptance of a diminished and broken image; no matter how use of the term is rationalized, laying claim to it in *any* manner is *self-defeating.*

Chapter 9

The Power of Words and Thought

Use of the N-word as a Conduit to an Inferior Mentality

"Thinking is usually a mixture of words, sentences, mental images and sensations. Thoughts are visitors, who visit the central station of the mind. They come, stay a while, and then disappear, making space for other thoughts. Some of these thoughts stay longer, gain power, and affect the life of the person thinking them."
~Remez Sasson

Is there power in thoughts and *words*? Can human lives be affected, altered and controlled by thoughts and *words*? Contrary to what many Black folks believe, the answer is *yes*. A vibratory energy lives in all thoughts, and the greater the emotional force behind words, the more power they have to affect lives, fates and destinies. Those who have benefited from the power of prayer understand the truth in that statement.

The subconscious mind is a receptacle where emotions, feelings and thoughts are harbored. Depending on whether the power emulating from this receptacle is positive or negative will be the determining factor as to how one's day-to-day living unfolds. Personalities, such as Anthony Robbins, Les Brown, Denis Waitley, Zig Ziglar and many others have for years held motivational seminars preaching and advocating the power of positive thinking. They understand the power of the mind and how the stored negative or positive energy released from it can affect one's life simply based on the words and thoughts flowing through it.

As conveyed in the above opening sentiments, thought is a dynamic, living force—the most subtle, yet influential and powerful force that exists in the universe. The thought-world is more real than the physical universe, for humans have the ability to create and interpret their own reality based on their subconscious desires and beliefs.   When speaking to elders about life and the future, they may sometimes reply with "pray about it and speak it into existence." In interpreting the latter part of that statement, it means that one can think of a certain situation or thing so much so, that they actually will, or think, that particular thing into existence. Thoughts are living things. Every change in thought is accompanied by vibration of its matter—meaning one's thoughts tend to surface in and direct one's behavior or actions.

Aside from words used relative to the occult, there is not a word in existence with the negative destructive power as that of the n-word. It is a word that over time has mistakenly been taken to be nothing more than a racial slur. Nothing could be further from the truth. This word is heavily laden with a psychological impediment. It serves as a self-generating and self-refueling reinforced psychosomatic conduit to an impecunious lifestyle to those who have been conditioned to accept its low vibratory rate of an all-consuming energy.

Until one is capable of taking control of their mind and thoughts, they are still a slave born into bondage, into a prison that they cannot taste, see or touch. Thinking and living an image that was long ago instilled in the psyche, an image that holds one hostage to a dastardly past, isn't conducive to independent thinking. In fact, it's validation of an enslaved mind.

For more than three centuries, African Americans were beaten, tortured and forced to absorb a self-hate, self-destructive, self-abasement and self-abnegation image of self. This image was then categorized as a n**ger. This is why the n-word is so detrimental to the Black community, yet still little realize that they are embracing an evil and negative energy; they dupe themselves into believing that it's just a word. To the contrary, the n-

word represents something far more than being *just* a word. Ultimately, *as a man thinketh, so he is.* In essence, one is who or what they believe themselves to be, and many Black Americans think of themselves as helpless, hopeless victims imprisoned in their own minds.

This mental confinement resulted in the contemporary Black race becoming psychological misfits unable to rise above mediocrity as a group. If the Black race continues to refuse to re-shape their minds and thinking regarding the n-word and other community-destructing behaviors—insisting on continual acceptance and embracement of the term n**ga, then the destiny and fate of a once dignified and truly glorious race of people will be assured and sealed into eternal damnation.

The Holy Bible references the power of words and thoughts on different accounts:

- "In the beginning was the *Word,* and the *Word* was with God, and the *Word* was God." (John 1:1)

- "And God said, Let there be light: and there was light."(Genesis 1:3)

- "And God said, Let the waters under the heaven be gathered together unto one place, and let the dry land appear: and it was so."(Genesis 1:9)

- "As a man thinketh... so he is." (Proverbs 23:7)

The Holy Bible also states:

- "For, whoever would love life and see good days must keep his tongue from evil and his lips from deceitful speech." (1 Peter 3:10)

- "He who guards his lips guards his life, but he who speaks rashly will come to ruin." (Proverbs 13:3)

The n-word is not the word of God; it is instead a satanic word from hell, there is absolutely nothing honorable about the word. Each time the word is spoken, it keeps alive the false-heartedness, dishonesty, and destructiveness black people have so long fallen victim to at the hands of the ruling class systemic and now some misguided, sycophant Black Americans as well.

Because of the vileness that lives in the term and the Black community's on-going use and acceptance of the idiom, the Black race on a whole instead of pointing fingers at their use of this immoral term, points fingers at White America for any misfortunes that may happen to come their way, refusing to acknowledge *the fact* that there is a negative and destructive energy flowing from this word—a word that in their naiveté—they work very hard at keeping alive.

The power of words is real and any word or term born of evil will only continue to bring about detrimental consequences. For any African American to acknowledge that there is such a thing as a n**ger is a travesty within itself. No such thing as a sub-human, 3/5 a person, bestial savage beast exists or ever existed which is how African American ancestors were looked upon as. In honor of African American's ascendants' sacred memories, the term should be unacceptable throughout the Black community in terms of labeling *anyone* as such. Black African Americans owe their ancestors at least that gem of *respect*.

African Americans who insist on toying with their minds through the use of the n-word may as well ingest poison and die slowly of toxic poisoning, for use of the n-word is tantamount to doing just exactly that from a psychological perspective.

Perhaps it is safe to say that all societal groups have their social ills, Black pathologies notwithstanding. However, Black America seems to have more than its share. Many pressing issues prevail in the Black community such as overcoming poverty, unemployment, children being born out of wedlock, public housing, food stamps, Black-on-Black crime, drug abuse, lack of self-respect, low esteem, use of the n-word and self-hatred. On the surface, it appears that the aforementioned issues are the major problems of Black America, but is that a true and accurate picture? Or, are these issues simply symptoms of the cause?

The contemporary African American is an enigma unto itself and the rest of the world. They represent some of the most skillful and athletic athletes in the world.

Black Americans are noteworthy talented artists renowned for their singing and musical capabilities, while still many others have risen to high places in other professions, arts and letters. With all their inventors, entrepreneurs, scholars, religious and political leaders, athletes, entertainers, teachers, and the inspiration of their rich African heritage, why aren't black people making more progress as a group? Why are Black schools declining? Why is the economic gap widening and not closing? Why are Black communities in decline—ravaged by crime, unemployment and despair?

How is it that their spending power exceeds many third world countries', but for some reason, there is no solution to solving the issue of Black economic independence? How is it that Black Americans have failed to realize the visions of Douglass, Garvey, Malcolm, and King when present day black people have the greatest opportunities available to them than has any other past generation?

On one hand, Blacks are in their current position because they have been socially engineered into their dilemma. Most Black African Americans have been systematically locked into a NO WIN situation. Black people, collectively, DO NOT own a significant amount of anything to be able to control their own lives. Whites in America control almost 100% of the income, wealth, power, resources, businesses, privileges and all levels of government.

Blacks comprise 13.6 percent of the U.S. population according to the 2010 Census, but account for only 1.4 percent of the top 1 percent of households by income. Whites are the overwhelming majority of the top 1 percent of households by income, comprising 96.2 percent. (Results were calculated from 2007 data from the Federal Reserve's Survey of Consumer Finances and the Tax Policy Center's tax table, The income cutoff to be a part of the top 1 percent was $646,195.)

Since 1860, inherited wealth has been locked into the white culture. This means that all the wealth and power in this country for the past 400 years has been systematically piloted into the hands of the majority white society, and, thus, Blacks come into the world with zero per cent wealth. In knowing this, it seems strongly impossible to compete against such overwhelming odds.

However, on the other hand, Blacks *help* to contribute to their oppression. Mentally-crippled black folks, who account for the majority of the Black community, use their poverty or victim card as a *free pass* to ignorance. They are content with proudly walking around poking out their chests, boasting how they *own* and have re-claimed the n-word (*n**ga/n**ger*); dismally to report, they claim this as their wealth. Such imbecility makes one want to regurgitate.

In order for mental enslavement to work and remain intact, the victims must be kept in their place. Clearly, many African Americans willingly and voluntarily accept their so-called place of that as n**gers/n**gahs. *Because* Blacks accept their appointed place as a n**ga and all the negative energy that comes along with it, (ie, Black-on-Black crime; rampant drug abuse, violence, and teen pregnancies; ill-education and financial disparity; etc.) oppressiveness will continue to haunt and cripple many in the Black community.

Looking at things from a different perspective according to a new study affluent African Americans are leaving industrial cities for the suburbs and the South shifting traditional lines between rich and poor.

Their migration is widening the income gap between whites and the inner-city black population who remain behind, while making African Americans *less united* as a group and subject to greater income disparities.

The census showed that cities such as Detroit, Chicago, Philadelphia, Cleveland and Milwaukee in particular saw increases in inequality, hurt by an exodus of middle-class minorities while lower-skilled blacks stayed in the cities.

Low-income blacks also slipped further behind. The share of black households ranking among the poorest poor - those earning less than $15,000 - climbed from 20 per cent to 26 per cent over the past decade; other race and ethnic groups posted smaller increases. [17]

At the same time, African-Americans making $200,000 or more a year were unchanged from 2000 at about 1.1 per cent, even after a deep recession.

Prince Georges County, Maryland—as of 2012—with a population of 881,138 is considered the wealthiest predominantly African-American county in the country, and as a result of its stratification, with the right kind of effort, has the potential of becoming the successful infrastructure that Tulsa City's Black Wall Street once was. [18]

It all hinges on whether or not the "wealthiest" status rises, remain the same or subside, and to what extend crime is held at bay and the school system enhances its effectiveness.

If you truly want to effect change, you must first change your way of thinking. You must free it from the restrictive thinking that holds you back. We are our thoughts, we cannot change anything if we cannot change the way we presently think. This is not man's law, but applies to a Law of the Universe.

Unfortunately, many of you are gophers you will go for anything. Someone tells you that you are the n-word—a n**ga—you go for it. If you don't stand for something you will fall for anything remaining forever on your knees moaning and groaning about unfair injustices.

The reality is that Black America is not benefiting from the blood, sweat and tears of their enslaved ancestors. Instead, the community seems to be walking around in perfect contentment with the claim to ownership of the n-word, a demeaning word that *dehumanized* their ancestors. Black African Americans, the hour is growing late the alarm clock is ringing but you continue to snooze on.

It is of political necessity for Blacks to be off center, off base, irrational and dumbed down so that the systemic can continue to do whatever it wants. No one in their *right* mind takes a word that degrades them, *dehumanized* their ancestors, and embraces it; no sane person would devise a thousand and one lame excuses in vain attempts to justify such bizarre behavior, excuses which would even insult the intelligence of a thinking *sixth grader*.

The Supreme Infinite Intelligence, known to some as God, gave each person a mind to use. By using such terms as the n-word, the greatest gift from this Supreme Intelligence is being wasted and disgraced; Blacks are allowing their gift to be controlled by someone else. Allowing someone else to control one's mind is a blatant refusal to use the sense blessed upon one at birth. Perhaps it is far easier to accept the definition of self that someone else has provided as opposed to actually *defining self* for self. In this ease of acceptance, know too that when one allows someone else to *define* them, they too open themselves up to whatever treatment the creator imposes upon them.

By using the n-word, the mind is enslaved to the

thinking of the ruling class. *As a person thinks, so they are.* That's the power of the human mind—no *if's, and's* or *but's* about it. The acts perpetuated upon the minds of the enslaved Africans are a story of human tragedy unequalled in the annals of humankind. The ramifications of that period have been passed down from generation to generation within the Black community not as a lesson to learn from but as a continual way of life and thinking.

What virtually all Black African Americans fail to understand is that the color of one's skin has *absolutely* nothing to do with what one experiences in life, although on the surface it may *appear* to be that way, however, all roads leads back to one's mindset. The mind is the most prized possession that one can possibly possess; when properly used, it is more valuable than money, diamonds, rubles, pearls, gold, silver, and any other form of currency or highly-valued jewel.

On the other hand, if the mind is improperly used, it can reduce a person to the level of a helpless, hopeless victim. The mind alone serves as the key to one's fate and destiny. The problem is the key can be used by *anyone.* Ultimately, if the owner chooses not to use the key for personal enlightenment, others will gladly use it, thus taking control of that individual's mind, fate and destiny. After all, if a person does not stand for something, they will surely fall for anything. In other words there is a price or penalty to pay for mental laziness. Control your own destiny or someone else will try for you.

The so-called oppressors associated the color *white* with being positive and superior, while the color *black* was associated with being negative and inferior. In other words, black people have been conditioned to be their own worst enemy; this is why they freely use the n-word because they associate black with negativity and do not even realize it.

Whatever habitual command a person gives their sub-conscious mind, the mind being the obedient servant, will obey. As one looks at their mahogany-complexioned skin, they see it as the source of their problems. On the flip side, this same person sees the white skin as a source of oppression, superiority, and opportunity. By thinking and believing this negativity, the subconscious carries out the misguided thinking as a so-called fact.

African Americans fail to realize the difference between them and their enslaved ancestors who didn't have the freedom to think for themselves, but that they as descendants have the power and freedom to do so but refuse, opening the door for the so-called oppressor to do their thinking for them. Ever since the enslaved Africans were first brought to America, a battle for control of the minds has waged, unbeknownst to present day African Americans.

Every time a black person refers to their child as *lil'* *n**ga*, thinking it's cool, chic and cute, they are further bruising, crippling, and sabotaging the development of a healthy psyche and self-image. The mind of a child is like a sponge, and by referring to that child as the n-word, the parent is following suit to their programming to raise their child as an eternal slave, same as how their parents unknowingly raised them.

The color of one's skin ultimately has nothing to do with their progress or complacency in this day and age. The fact that black people in this 21st century still refer to self and one another as the n-word is a dead giveaway that many still do not have control of their own minds. In order to have a better life here on earth, the physiology of the human mind must be understood and applied.

Learn to stop pointing fingers at the white man as he is no longer the primary problem; he simply is permitted to continue controlling the mind because of Black America's insistence and continual holding on to 18th century slave mentalities refusing to take control of their own minds.

That inaccuracy in thinking has black people believing that the white man is the primary issue. The white man can only keep the power and control if Black America allows it; use of the n-word is a prime example. Is the systemic guilty of mind control tactics to help keep African Americans in a particular mindset? Yes! However its effectiveness can be neutralized whenever one decides to take back control of their own mind.

Black Americans must turn their faces to the books and learn about the power of the human mind. African Americans must stop being mentally lazy and speaking out of ignorance or defending ideas they know absolutely nothing about. It is one thing to be ignorant because everyone is ignorant about something or another, but when led to the water trough of awareness and knowledge and one refuses to drink, instead electing to remain ignorant, that is inexcusable and unforgiveable.

Stop thinking like a slave! Surrendering to self-chosen ignorance is self-defeating and contemptible. As Confucius once said, "[t]hinking without learning is dangerous."

A greater appreciation for what the mind can achieve and overcome must be enacted. The minds of black people are just as fertile as any other; however, failing to understand the seriousness and consequences of what's fed into the subconscious precipitates a recipe for cultural genocide and a never-ending menticide. As Morpheus said to Neo in the motion picture film the

Matrix, "I'm trying to free your mind, Neo. But I can only show you the door. You're the one that has to walk through it."

Ninety percent or more of Black Americans are still mentally enslaved. Black Americans must take back control of their minds or forever remain a slave. A n**ger/n**ga is a created manmade thing or image. Denouncing the term is an important step in mental liberation and serves as the key ingredient of power to self-create.

The proposal presented is to initiate the process of undoing or reversing ideas and concepts which have been programmed into the minds of many Black African Americans over a 400-year period. This programming has caused many to adopt a belief system that has resulted in their loss of contact with that which is real, factual, historically and spiritually-sound.

Control your own mind or someone else will.

Johann Wolfgang von Gothe, 1749-1832, once stated that "NONE ARE MORE HOPELESSLY ENSLAVED THAN THOSE WHO FALSELY BELIEVE THEY ARE FREE."

Black African Americans, from the first day their ancestors set foot on this land, have been hoodwinked and bamboozled in so many countless different ways that it's tragic to even think about it; and all of these acts were carried out as a way of keeping the Black race off-balanced, off-centered and discombobulated. Slave drivers spoke words of hate into the minds of black people which still sit strongly at the forefront of black people's minds and subconsciously drive their actions. In order to effectively undo the brainwashing process, Blacks must learn to speak only and dwell on words filled with positivity, peace and progression in their daily lives; the n-word does not fit this bill.

If you're thinking like everyone else—and using the n-word—then you aren't thinking. Other than committing

suicide, you don't get to choose how you are going to die, or when. But you *can choose* how you are going to live, right now.

Chapter 10

Who are *YOU?*
What is *Your* Name?

"Only when lions have historians will hunters cease to be heroes."
~African Proverb

As we approach the 21st century, we can no longer permit the holocaust of African enslavement to define our conceptions of ourselves...In fact, we must begin with a re-Africanization (sic) process that includes rediscovery, redefinition and revitalization.
~Harold Charles

Olmec Civilization Pre-Classical Mesoamerica from c. 1200 BCE to c. 400 BCE

Throughout the writing of this narrative, great focus has been on use of the n-word. The n-word and its use have been pegged as one of the most significant causes that have led to the continued demise and degradation of the Black community.

Although this argument is still withstanding, indeed, a larger issue and *root* cause is at hand; this issue penetrates even deeper than the n-word. The unanswered question or standing issue of *"WHO ARE WE (Black /African Americans)?"* has long plagued the community and been the primary reason why the Black race cannot "get right."

Not understanding who one truly is leads to confusion in every other aspect of one's life, for that group has no direction or clear path to follow. If one is sure of who they are—good or bad—in fullness and truth, they will be better able to make decisions, realize what they will and will not stand for, as well as confirm to self and others what they do and do not represent.

Often times, the question has been raised as to what Black Americans should refer to themselves—is it *Black*, *African American*, *Negro* or exactly what? Obviously, the race is in total disarray over this identity crisis, and there is an explanation for it...

Whites have taken it upon themselves to classify all groups into racial categories. However, the only groups who play this game are Black and white folks. Asians do not refer to themselves as *Yellows*, nor parade around chanting "Yellow Power;" the same goes for the Hispanics who do not make a habit of referring to themselves as *Browns*, nor do Indians refer to themselves as *Redskins* or Red anything.

Not only did the classification *Black* come from Whites, but terms such as *Colored*, *Negro*, and *n**ger* did as well. All were created with a particular purpose: when Whites made a distinction between *White* and *Black*, they painted being black as inferior and evil, while white was considered pure, superior and good. Refusing to remain voluntary victims of this classification, African Americans of the '60's reclaimed the term *black*, embracing and acknowledging the positive aspects of what it means to be *Black*.

This same attempt is being made in hip-hop as they try to use the same argument in a so-called re-claiming of the n-word (n**ga) today.

However, this effort is futile because the terms are from two different worlds. One cannot help being "black"

James Brown album "Say It Loud" reflects the indomitable spirit of the 60s along with the slogan "Black is Beautiful".

because one cannot choose the color of their skin, one is just born that way. As such, being *black* must be embraced in order to accept and appreciate one's self fully. On the other hand, there is no such thing as a n**ger/n**ga. The n-word was a term applied to Black people by man, not God, and its intent and purpose was to dehumanize a race of people. Nothing innately sinister lives in the color black; however, the same cannot be said for the venomous and evil n-word (n**ger). Truthfully, to be candid, Asian people aren't yellow, Hispanics aren't brown, and Indians aren't red. African Americans are not black—brown perhaps, but not black. Caucasians are not white; they may be lacking in color, but they certainly are not white. The only "white" people are albinos.

For an in-depth understanding of classifications in America as well as to see without doubt how the systemic controls and manipulates based on what's good for the majority class, take a look at the Census Bureau's classification of race groups:

Directive #15 RACE AND ETHNIC STANDARDS FOR FEDERAL STATISTICS AND ADMINISTRATIVE REPORTING (adopted May 12, 1977)

These classifications should not be interpreted as being scientific or anthropological in nature; these are racial classifications according to the USA standards:

DEFINITIONS:

The basic racial and ethnic categories for Federal statistics and program administrative reporting are defined as follows:

- ***American Indian or Alaskan Native****: A person having origins in any of the original people of North America, and who maintains cultural identification through tribal affiliation or community recognition.* **Note***: No reference to color.*

- ***Asian or Pacific Islander:*** *A person having origins in any of the original people of the Far East, Southeast Asia, the Indian subcontinent, or the Pacific Islands. This area includes for example, China, India, Japan, Korea, the Philippine Islands, and Samoa.* **Note***: No reference to color.*

- ***Black:*** *A person having origins in any of the black racial groups of Africa.* **Note**: *The reference to black racial groups omitting any ties to a nation; and no reference to Blacks as the* original *people of any particular nation in Africa, which makes the categorization of a color as opposed to a nationality highly significant.*

- **Hispanic:** *A person of Mexican, Puerto Rican, Cuban, Central or South American or other Spanish culture or origin <u>regardless</u> of race.* **Note:** *No reference to color.*

- **<u>White</u>:** *A person having origins in any of the **original** people of Europe, North Africa, or the Middle East.* **Note:** *The categorization of color is done with a particular purpose in mind, as is the reference to Black; names are of the essence of the game of power and control.*

The history of the world is the history of humanity and the roots of civilization. The old civilizations had their greatest accomplishments in the proximity of their origins. For Africans, this is the North African, Ethiopian, Malian, Songhai and Ghanian areas. The sands of time have destroyed only the body of ancient Egypt Civilizations; its spirit survives in the lore and memory of its primordial golden age race.

Euro-centricity teaches there is no connection of Blacks' enhancement with history and culture--factors which proclaim the humanity of an individual. In order to ensure they can lay claim to any and everything in the world as being theirs, per the definition above, Whites claim to be the *original* people of *North Africa.* How can that be the case? The continent of Africa was originally comprised of *all* Black people. Scientific discoveries are constantly being made to validate this truth. [14]

Reparations

The question about reparations surfaces often when discussing self-awareness among the Black populous as many are perplexed as to why Black African Americans never received their promised 40 acres and a mule. Ever since subjugated Black Africans first set foot on the American land, the systemic has been hoodwinking and bamboozling Black African American people left and right; to this very day, this is still happening.

Reparations are brought to light in this discussion because the answer to the question "Who are we?" may be linked to the reasoning as to why African Americans have never been able to receive their fair portion.

President Obama has quietly granted reparations to some groups of people, some of whom were included in the stimulus package; however, Blacks were excluded from this cash out and perhaps always will be—no matter who is president. Although in year 2010, Obama did grant Black farmers $1.25 billion in reparations, they have yet to receive one penny of it.

To say that this issue is a challenging one is an understatement. Arguments for and against providing reparations to Black descendants of slaves are plentiful. Suffice it to say that a formal acknowledgement and apology for the inhumanity of slavery has never been issued by the U. S. government. The effects of slavery and the racial prejudice that went hand in hand with it, even after slavery was outlawed, put Blacks at a significant socioeconomic disadvantage: from jump street, Blacks had fewer opportunities to obtain a good education, descent-paying jobs, and a solid opportunity at acquiring economic security. Though some Blacks have been able to overcome the dilemma, most have not.

Congressman John Conyers of Michigan, recognizing the complexity and sensitivity of this issue, has introduced legislation each year since 1989 that would establish a commission to study reparations proposals. Though there are many pros and cons around the question of issuing Blacks reparations, could one of the main points of contention be that because *Black, Negro* or *Colored* is not *linked* to a nation of any kind including the term "African American," that this is one of the main reasons Black African Americans are being deprived of any sort of reparation? The term *African American* is in of itself a misnomer considering the fact that Africa is a continent and not a nation.

Another point of contention is how the 13th Amendment is worded:

SLAVERY AND INVOLUNTARY SERVITUDE

THIRTEENTH AMENDMENT

SECTION 1. Neither slavery nor involuntary servitude, except as a punishment for crime whereof the party shall have been duly convicted, shall exist within the United States, or any place subject to their jurisdiction.

SECTION 2. Congress shall have power to enforce this article by appropriate legislation.

Does the very use of the word *involuntary servitude* leave the door open to *voluntary* servitude? And if so, who would volunteer for such a status? The answer may be very surprising.

Have Black African Americans *voluntarily* enslaved themselves by being categorized as *Black, Negro, Colored and/or African American* on their birth certificates? Go back to the census statistics and see if a picture doesn't unfold. The groups that Obama granted reparations to are all linked to a nation one way or another. The only group listed in the census not definitely linked to a nation is the Black category. A color is not a link to a nation, history or culture. When it comes to legal means, regardless to the US Census Bureau's classifications, Whites do not refer to themselves as *White*, maybe Caucasian, Anglo, etc. but not white unless in some way it proves to be to their benefit.

On the other hand, when it comes to legal means, Black African Americans are the only group who generally refers to itself by color; thus, are they unknowingly, and perhaps *voluntarily* cementing their status as detached, wandering slaves, and a people not linked to a nation—even though they may refer to themselves as simply African American? The term African American is in of itself a catch-22, there is a designated history, heritage and culture connected to the term and it begins with 17th century America. Connection to an African nation is vital and imperative.

There are some who may say that Black African Americans' nationality is American, but it tells them absolutely nothing about who they are? America is a melting pot, whereas, all groups—with the exception of the American Indian—heritage and culture extend beyond its boundaries.

The ultimate take-away here is that—unlike Mexican-American, Korean-American, Filipino-American, etc., which are ties to a nation—if the term Black/African American cannot be identified or tied back to a nation, where does this leave them?

The Significance of Heritage

Humans are free moral agents; because humans can determine their future to a great degree, humankind is often deluded into thinking the past has no impact on their future. To the contrary, choices and past events have very profound and long-lasting impacts on any decision made; therefore, all decisions or choices made now are done so in the context of the past. As such, as White America already knows, and Black African Americans must come to know and understand, is that by limiting their history and culture to experiences in America, Black America is unknowingly narrowing or shortening its future potential.

Heritage, whether it be national, cultural, or familial, is

an endowment of unique sets of historical knowledge; but foremost, heritage is a person's history. Heritage is responsible for how a person came to be; it is a very large part of who and what one is as a person. It essentially helps to identify one's "starting position" in life. Heritage can also heavily determine what feats one has the potential to overcome and become in life; therefore, in that sense, it can help *define* what path one may want take in life.

The sense of identity gained from studying heritage will help to explain to self and others the essence of that individual and their own spirit. Heritage lives deep within and can be called upon for personal motivation, endurance, and encouragement in trying times. The thinking: "ancestors were able to overcome more trying and testing situations, and because their blood courses through my veins, I have the power and spirit within me too to overcome the matter."

Heritage is an inheritance better than money or property, something that should not be minimized, lost or forgotten. Though Black African Americans' heritage was stolen, the good news is that it can be taken back; this task is the sole responsibility of Black America. To continue to discard or think nothing of the significance of one's heritage bespeaks of inertia and indolence.

What value is an instruction manual to a complex machine if it is left in the packing material or thrown away? None! But when the manual is read, the knowledge will be encapsulated in the mind and used. In that moment, the greatest value of a blueprint will be realized. Heritage is the blueprint that will help one navigate around certain pitfalls and continue to build upon legacies of greatness. There are those whose sole aim and purpose is to relegate Black African Americans to a culture and heritage of subjugation and jungle life—robbing them of their *true* legacy.

Many Black African Americans fail to realize that cultural roots are the foundation of uniqueness. Knowing one's origins, traditions, and customs creates the root of finding ones' self. *It's imperative that Black America stop giving someone else the power to change them from the descendant nature of ancient Golden Age forefathers.* Culture plays an important role in shaping principles and morals. Culture is what ties a community together and makes it distinctive. Culture also helps to distinguish, define, and ultimately enrich a person's life.

To be cut off from one's heritage would be the same as renouncing one's birthright and betraying ancestors, to eternally remain mentally enslaved. Culture is greatly influential; it is an invisible bond that ties a community together. Black Americans must individually ponder and reflect on their origins, who they are as a person today, and clarify their beliefs only for self. Self-reflection is the first step of self-discovery.

The Moorish-American Treaty of Peace Friendship of 1787

The evidence of Africans in America before Columbus is an important aspect of the individual's and group's self-identity. Their pre-Columbus existence provides a strong sense of a nation-oriented position, belongingness and historical value. This basic idea of nationality creates the venue by which one begins to take unwavering pride in one's national parentage identity. Self-awareness and identity strongly serves as the basis for high self-esteem. The degree of power, success and social standing is critically important to the national citizenry/members well-being, sense of security and purpose. [15]

In 1787, America signed a treaty with Morocco. It seems as though when Columbus found his way to America, he came across more than just Indians. He also came across some Black folks known as Moors. One will find in their history quest for knowledge and self-awareness that Moors inhabited the American land before the so-called Native American Indian. Thus, bi-racial Black-Indians roamed the unknown land far before Africans were brought to the new-world shackled and chained.

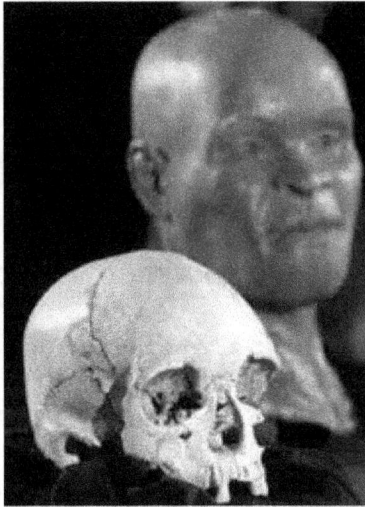

Skull of a young black female. The oldest discovered skull in the Americas. Believed to be 12,000 years old. [19]

At some point between 1774 and 1779, White America decided they wanted to categorize the Moors as *Black, Negro* and *Colored*. Morocco, who laid claim to the vast land before the Europeans ever knew of its existence, entered into a treaty with America protecting the Moors to prevent them from being classified as *Black, Negro* or *Colored*. As a result, this non-classification provided Moors the same rights, privileges and protection as that of White people. See: *Negro Law of South Carolina;*

The Status of the Negro, his Rights and Disabilities

Chapter 1

Sec. 4. The term negro is confined to slave Africans, (the ancient Berbers) and their descendants. It does not embrace the free in-habitants of Africa, such as the Egyptians, Moors, or the negro Asiatics, such as the Lascars. Scot

Perhaps, this is one of the reasons that whites refuse to classify themselves by a group name and, instead, by color. Even if the Moors were placed into the same social class as whites, the whites strongly desired to still keep themselves separated or differentiated from the rest; the only key factor separating all of these "Americans" was color.

Ultimately, the difference between the Moors of the 7th Century and the Black African Americans of the 21st Century is that the Moors were masters of their own fate and destiny. The Moor's state of mind was free from the violation of forced subjugation; unencumbered, unpolluted from the abyss of mental enslavement.

Understand, the American Institutionalized Systemic knows the real truth, and as contradictory or senseless as their actions are, they serve as proof that the system is continually working day and night to keep the rest of America and the world in the dark regarding real world history. White America basically does whatever it takes to maintain the façade, and no one really questions their motives. Mostly, all, including non-Blacks, have been conditioned in one way or another to believe that only truth pours from the lips of the oppressor. The Black race, most notably, suffers the gravest from this line of thinking and their apathy when it comes to learning the truth for themselves.

The systemic knows how important self-awareness is to either advancing or holding the Black community in its current stagnant and broken place. Black America must understand their true status and equality. Once Black America on the whole develops a healthy self-image founded on true self-awareness, which will come about only through re-educating self in real world history, the race at large will be able to lay to rest any and all suffocating remnants of the past.

Once Black America decides to educate itself, about itself, books and narratives basically begging Blacks to respect themselves won't have to be written. As one becomes wise and the veil is removed from their eyes, they will grow a level of self-awareness that won't allow them to accept anything beyond the truth. In this process, the love of all things negative will sub-side, including the n-word.

Epilogue:

A Final Call to Action and Resolve of the N-word Dilemma

to go back and take

SANKOFA:

A West African word meaning to retrieve the past in order to live in the future.

The entire Black American population owes it to self and their forefathers to unearth the truth. Black African Americans have been bamboozled and hoodwinked long enough. To determine a real future for Black America, the entire race of people must learn about and embrace their past far back across the water to use that as a foundation and a source of life for future progress. Black America must not wait to learn about Black history when it is convenient for the rest of America, but must remain owners of their own enlightenment, keepers of their own achievements, and missionaries of their own salvation. Equally important is that the foundation of self-respect be established.

Self-hatred is synonymous with use of the n-word; therefore, as the first step towards laying the foundation of longevity, prosperity, and true enlightenment, the n-word has to be eradicated. Can change come about overnight? Of course not! If the right effort to bring about change were to be applied this very moment, the best hope is that some semblance of change would be recognized within two to three generations. To overcome 400 years of mind control will take some time for the seed of change to take root and grow, but the seed must first be planted and watered daily. It is this first step that will initiate the process towards building a foundation of self-respect. There is no shortcut; the foundation of self-respect is a prerequisite for real change.

The Black community on a whole must discard the 18th century slave mentality, become self-sufficient, and regain control of its own destiny. It can be done; it's been proven: Blacks achieved this feat during the early 1920's (Tulsa City, Oklahoma) and in the '60's. This same change can once again be attained. To affect *true* change, Blacks must initiate and be the change that they seek. When Blacks think and act in a positive fashion *as a group*, positive things happen exponentially.

The enemy is deeply entrenched within and outside the race. This means that Black America must face up to the fact that they are part of the problem and acknowledge that they have obstacles to overcome that are experienced by no other group.

Religion has its place and it's commendable that so much emphasis is placed on preparation for life in the hereafter, yet that same energy and concern for survival in the here and now is trivialized. While the so-called self-appointed messengers of God are surviving quite comfortably here on earth off their followers' 10%, these same followers are urged to seek their kingdoms on earth in the hereafter.

One thing is certain: if an individual doesn't design their own life plan, chances are they'll fall into someone else's plan. And guess what that plan or ration is for the follower? Not much! The planner is too busy looking out for themselves at the follower's expense.

Each person has the ability to think, create desires and ideas of their own. This is why each person—from an Almighty source—was given a brain in the first place. Fail to use it, and you simply suffer the consequences. The Universe smiles with favor upon the mentally strong and has nothing but disdain for the mentally weak.

Mind development is why the formative years of the young are so important. Without proper guidance, young spongy minds more than likely will be ingested with all sorts of negativity. They then grow up into adulthood with these habitual thoughts that are thoroughly ingrained into their sub-conscious minds. It is habitual thoughts that the sub-conscious listens to and carries out. Habits are hard to break, and the sub-conscious is highly resistant to change, making it difficult for adults to successfully affect change in their lives.

Best analogy is that of a person trying to lose weight and keep that weight off. If that person's conscious and sub-conscious mind is in sync, they will successfully lose weight and keep it off. However, if the sub-conscious has a different thought in mind or reluctance about successfully losing the weight, the weight will be back. What most people fail to realize is that in the long run, the sub-conscious is a determining factor in any successes or failures. In an unguarded moment when a habitual thought re-enters the sub-conscious, that is the command the conscious mind and body are going to always follow.

The youth are the wave of the future, but their *young*

impressionable minds—which is key as to how their habitual way of thinking is molded—must be properly nurtured for any chance and hope of *real change*.

The journey ahead will test the intestinal fortitude of the Black African American and its will to survive as a group. The challenge that now awaits the Black African American is to overcome centuries of coercive persuasion. This task will likely prove to be Black America's greatest challenge in this era of perpetual crisis; but the good news is that overcoming this obstacle or successfully completing this task is *totally possible*.

Consider the famous case (1974) of Patty Hearst's brainwashing. An American newspaper heiress, socialite, actress, and convicted bank robber was kidnapped by a group of young political radicals calling themselves the Symbionese Liberation Army. She had been confined and locked up in a dark closet for more than three months subjected to harsh mind control trauma. This led to her committing a number of bank robberies and killings with the group. She was convicted of bank robbery despite her defense that she had been a victim of the Stockholm Syndrome, where hostages develop sympathy for their captors and tend to support them. On the theory that she was not responsible for her actions because her indoctrination into the group did indeed qualify as *brainwashing,* her sentence was commuted by President Jimmy Carter. Hearst was later pardoned by President Bill Clinton.

Reality is such that equal rights and equal justice will *never* come from the powers that be and/or granted as an act of grace. Instead, this leveling will only be established by Black America's position of power and influence. That unwavering and real power is born from a UNITED and mentally-LIBERATED people engaged in great and vast undertakings of their own. Mental liberation and racial unity can lead to *economic independence* which serves as a prerequisite to true equality and respect.

It should be pointed out that all other groups have racial unity, which is normal and not a form of racism; however, Black African Americans are not encouraged to unite, quite the contrary, are discouraged from doing so and any attempts at it is inappropriately looked upon as racism. It remains to be seen if Black America ever wake up from its comatose state of mind and see through the Divide and Conquer tactic that from day one has been applied to them leaving them brain dead to the significance of United We Stand! Divided We Fall!

" If you wish to move mountains tomorrow, you must
start by lifting stones today."
— African Proverbs

About the Author

H. Lewis Smith attended Cal State University Los Angeles, and for more than two decades has been a student of metaphysics, focusing his studies on idioms and meanings, analyzing the psychological impact of words, their energy and vibratory effects on the human mind. Smith is the Founder & president of the United Voices for a Common Cause, Inc. and author of *Bury that Sucka: A Scandalous Love Affair with the N-word.*

Suggested Reading

Blackmon, Douglas A. (2009) – *Slavery By Another Name*

Byrne, Rhonda (2006) - The Secret

Clarke, John Henrik (1994) – *Who Betrayed the African World Revolution*

Davidson, Basil (1991) – *African Civilization Revisited*

DeGruy, Joy (2005) – *Post Traumatic Slave Syndrome*

Diop, Cheikh Anta (1974) – *African Origin of Civilization*

Diop, Cheikh Anta (1991) – *Civilization or Barbarism*

Feimster, Crystal (2009) – *Southern Horrors: Women and the Politics of Rape and Lynching*

Hilliard, Asa G. (1987) – *Testing African American Students*

Houston, Drusilla D. (1926) – *Wonderful Ethiopians of the Ancient Cushite Empire*

James, George G.M. (1992) – *Stolen Legacy*

Johnson, Umar A. (2013) – *Psycho-Academic Holocaust: The Special Education and ADHD War Against Black Boys*

Obenga, Theophile (2006) – *African Philosophy: During the Period of the Pharaohs*

Murphy, Joseph 1963 - The power of Your Subconscious Mind

Murphy, Joseph (1955) - Believe in Yourself

Murphy, Joseph (1965) - The Amazing Laws of Cosmic Mind Power

Rajshekar, V.T. (1981) – *The Black Untouchables of India*

Rashidi, Runoko & Sertima, Ivan V. (1987) – *African Presence in Early Asia*

Sertima, Ivan (1976) – *They Came Before Columbus*

Smith, H. Lewis (2005) – *Bury that Sucka: A Scandalous Love Affair With the N-word*

Walker, David (1829) - Appeal

Williams, Chancellor (1992) – *The Destruction of Black Civilization*

Williams, Richard (2010) – *They Stole It But You Must Return It*

Woodson, Carter G. (1933) – *The Mis-Education of the Negro*

Notes and Sources

1. Spartacus Educational:
   http://www.spartacus.schoolnet.co.uk/USASbr
   eeding.htm

2. Williams, Richard - *They Stole It But You Must Return It,* 2010. Heme Publishing

3. Hill, Pascoe G. *Fifty Days Onboard a Slave Vessel,* 1993

4. Racism: A History [2007] 3/3, -
   https://www.youtube.com/watch?v=oCJHJWa
   NL-g

5. DeGruy, Joy, Dr. - *Post Traumatic Slave Syndrome,* 2005. Joy DeGruy Publications Inc.

6. Return to Glory Part 1:
   https://www.youtube.com/watch?v=BCHPuqtj
   CRU

7. Great Kings and Queens of Africa by AnheuserBuschCorp [2012]:
   https://www.youtube.com/watch?v=AUAh

8. Williams, Chancellor - *The Destruction of Black Civilization,* 1971

9. The African Moors In Spain:
   https://www.youtube.com/watch?v=16KQsMjC
   kbc

10. John Horse and the Black Seminoles the First Black Rebels to Beat American Slavery: http://www.johnhorse.com/

11. Black African History and Black Empires: https://www.youtube.com/watch?v=WKOWERczykU

12. Williams, Chancellor - *The Destruction of Black Civilization*, 1971

13. Black Africa History and Black Empires You Were Never Told About: https://www.youtube.com/watch?v=WKOWERczykU&list=PLo89PW71-nAfdiONLJ9cEHn11Nnb90SXy

14. The Incredible Human Journey, posted by Carlos Noetzold http://www.youtube.com/watch?v=vwa6o-s1Yvs August 2011

15. Sertima, Ivan - *They Came Before Columbus,* 1976

16. http://en.wikipedia.org/wiki/Arab_slave_trade

17. http://www.huffingtonpost.com/2011/12/08/income-inequality_n_1136256.html

18. http://sfbayview.com/2011/what-happened-to-black-wall-street-on-june-1-1921/

19. Untold Black History: "Blacks" Were the 1st Americas https://www.youtube.com/watch?v=1N_2eMlEsh8

Index